THE STORY OF ECCLES CARAVANS

ANDREW JENKINSON

AMBERLEY

Dedicated to the Riley family, whose forward thinking would bring pleasure to many.

First published 2017

Amberley Publishing
The Hill, Stroud,
Gloucestershire, GL5 4EP

www.amberley-books.com

Copyright © Andrew Jenkinson, 2017

The right of Andrew Jenkinson to be identified as the Authors
of this work has been asserted in accordance with the
Copyrights, Designs and Patents Act 1988.

All rights reserved. No part of this book may be reprinted
or reproduced or utilised in any form or by any electronic,
mechanical or other means, now known or hereafter invented,
including photocopying and recording, or in any information
storage or retrieval system, without the permission in writing
from the Publishers.

Map illustration by Thomas Bohm, User Design, Illustration and Typesetting.

ISBN: 978 1 4456 6866 6 (print)
ISBN: 978 1 4456 6867 3 (ebook)

British Library Cataloguing in Publication Data.
A catalogue record for this book is available from the British Library.

Typeset in 10pt on 13pt Celeste.
Origination by Amberley Publishing.
Printed in the UK.

Contents

	Foreword	4
Chapter One	The Eccles Caravan and Motorhome Are Born	5
Chapter Two	Eccles Develops New Models and Lead in Caravan Mass Production	31
Chapter Three	Eccles, a New Era	51
Chapter Four	Eccles Leads into the '80s and Beyond	74

Foreword

Eccles is a name that's been around since 1919. Little did its owners, the Riley family, ever realise that the company would become such an innovator and would survive a World War, and a good few downturns in the economy too! Not only would they run a successful business from 1919 to early 1960, they would also commercialise the idea of a car-pulled caravan, and also develop the motorhome concept. They invented the over-run braking system for touring caravans, which was soon copied and became the standard by the late 1920s.

Eccles would build all types of specials, from luxury showman vans to commercial special units for mobile displays. Eccles also built the first UK fifth-wheeler caravan and four-wheeled caravans. Eccles was the name that dominated the '20s and '30s into the mid-'40s and '50s under the Riley family. By the '60s they were back again with innovative design and construction under the Ci brand. By 1983 they were under a new Ci Group again with some industry-leading designs, and then from 1993 they were under Sprite Leisure, who would be purchased by the Swift Group in late 1994.

Swift, over the last twenty-three years, has carried the Eccles name forward and, with all the heritage the brand has behind it, the Eccles touring caravan is one of the best-known names in caravanning, and not just in the UK either. The Eccles story tells of how through sheer determination and early marketing it projected the car-pulled trailer caravan as a new leisure interest, and also how it sowed the seeds for the motorhome industry years later.

CHAPTER ONE

The Eccles Caravan and Motorhome Are Born

The beginning of the Rileys' involvement in motorhomes began as far back as 1913 with the idea of converting a car to be able to be used as sleeping accommodation. The Riley father and son team W. A. Riley Senior and W. J. Bill Riley built a caravan-styled body onto a Talbot chassis. Helped by their gardener, the project was seen to completion and the first coachbuilt motorhome was developed. Its overall styling was more like that of a commercial delivery van; one onlooker described it as a 'baker's delivery van'! On tests it didn't quite prove a success with faults occurring, but the design was basic and needed to be more finely tuned.

In early 1914, the Rileys' yet-unbranded motorhome received attention of the *Autocar* motoring magazine, which already had become a respected journal for those interested

The first Eccles motorhome. The design and build was done in 1914 by the Riley father and son team – the gardener leant a hand too!

in the latest happenings in the world of motor vehicles. The outcome was that the Rileys would be approached by a coachbuilder in Birmingham after reading the article, with the idea that a patent would be issued and purchased by the coachbuilder so that the idea could be further developed. The Rileys, however, decided that they would only allow permission for the motorhome design to be used.

With the First World War beginning, pressure for war work meant that the coachbuilder had to stall any further work on the motorhome idea. Riley Junior was to join up with the Royal Flying Corps, later re-named the RAF, where he experienced the usage of trailer ambulances. He noted how relatively easy it was for these car-pulled trailers to be used to sleep in and adapted to fit a cooker and seating and easy to make a bed to sleep in. After the years of war, young Riley, demobbed from service, joined up with his father to pool their resources and look at going into business. Father wanted young Bill to join him mainly because he had been getting into mischief, so Riley Senior had him in the business to keep him in check. We don't know what he used to get up to, but by today's standards it was probably very little!

They then spotted in a local Birmingham newspaper company operating lorries for haulage work, which was looking for extra cash to be injected to grow the business. This seemed like a good opening into the world of business that would expand over the years as more roads were built and goods transported by this more modern means. They contacted the owner, who was a Mr Eccles, and their proposals were accepted. Along with the deal, they gave the company a new name – Eccles Motor Transport Ltd (registered 21 March 1919).

The company was based in a rather derelict corner house that had with it some dilapidated cottages. Roughly, the premise consisted of 3,000 sq ft and was situated at Gosta Green, Birmingham. The investment was looking promising at all, especially when

Bill Riley Senior (inset) and the original Eccles premises at Gosta Green, pre-development.

the so-called fleet of vehicles was more closely inspected! They were past their best and needed extensive repairs to be carried out to keep in business.

The company premises needed good investment and, impressively pooling every available penny they had, the Rileys invested £6,000 into the business, which was a big chunk of cash back in 1919! The so-called fleet of three old tractors had been used for wartime haulage and to say the least, servicing hadn't been a priority! With the wartime contracts now also at an end, the three vehicles were basically idle. With this dilemma facing the business, a sales drive to get new business was pursued. The old vehicles were repaired and, in the meantime, the company purchased two new haulage lorries.

Being purchased with loans, the now eight-man team with drivers and mechanics were slowly getting new business. Mr Eccles ran the office while young Riley was a manager. However, the business wasn't making much money, with a sales turnover of just £3,500; plus, the old cottages that had become clearly unsafe had to be demolished too. The company then built a Belfast roof design construction – a design from the 1860s that consisted of a large-span roof with supports in the middle to strengthen it – to replace the demolished cottages and at least allow more covered yard area.

Struggling with turnover and repaying the debts, the Rileys were keen to try and make money in another area; this is when the idea of the motorhome came back to play. Riley Senior decided to use the old, large kitchen in the house at Gosta Green to build another prototype, but this time he had some improvements to make it more sellable. Riley Junior had other ideas; although he liked his father's concept, he was keen to try a car-pulled design. His father thought the idea was not as commercial as the motorised caravan design. However, the Riley team agreed that both could be designed and built in this one small area of the premises. Riley Junior though was keen to show how his trailer caravan would be received – a little father and son competition would kick in!

The first 1919 number one Eccles trailer caravan was primitive but was soon developed within a couple of years to a small range.

Work began on both, with hours spent after working building the two prototypes. It was also a gamble, because the two leisure vehicles were actually pioneers in design and would also need to be sold and marketed as a new 'hobby'. Little did the pair then realise that they were to be the founders of a new industry that would encompass most of the globe in the years to come. The next move was to be how to display and promote the new ideas. At the 1919 Olympia Motor Show, the Rileys tried to get a space for a stand but it was virtually impossible, so the next move was to hire a garage nearby and display the pair during the show.

The two Eccles designs began to attract a lot of interest as visitors looked over them. It was one thing having lots of interest though – what the team really needed was buyers, and that wasn't as forthcoming as they had hoped. Then a lady was spotted looking over the trailer caravan. After what seemed a long time of looking over the caravan, the request for her name resulted in a reply of 'Lady Dowager Viscountess Rhonadda' – a multi-millionairess. The first sale made, plenty of interest was shown for the two units and, though no strong sales resulted, the pair decided to bite the bullet and actually begin producing trailer caravans as well as motorhomes.

The first Eccles tourers were built using a chassis designed and built by the Rileys. They had a primitive leather coupling but this was soon replaced by a patented shock-absorbing cantilever coupling. Rolled steel sheets and soldered seems with interior oak panelling was how the early Eccles were constructed. The tourers were taking all the interest but the Rileys still had to sell the idea as the Gosta Green factory had caravans being built that were yet to be sold. Trying to sell the idea to the public would see Riley Junior taking a trailer caravan on a tour to call at garages to see if he could drum up business. He also found design weaknesses and rectified these in later production models.

Within a couple of years the early '20s saw the Eccles round cornered models appear such as this 8 ft No. 15 model.

What did come out of the sales and marketing push was that interest and purchases were made for hiring. This new hobby was definitely going to be for the car owning upper classes. Towing wasn't seen as a major issue but with one initial model, very quickly new models were to be developed along with new designs that were based loosely on the old horse-drawn profiles with lantern roofs, classing these as De-Luxe models. Lengths would be available from 8 ft to 12 ft as layout ideas were developed.

Sales did begin to pick up with hirers such as the Holiday Caravan Company, based at Oxford, who found hiring a good way to sell. With the motoring press picking up interest too, Eccles received more publicity. Articles were written on the joys and freedom and the health advantages motor caravanning gave. Prices ranged from £105 to £250 fully furnished. The Rileys were now getting enquires from businesses that wanted to sell as well as hire the Eccles caravans; Woolley Brothers in Bristol with the London Caravan Co., for example, were early Eccles dealers/distributors in the 1920s.

Orders were taken for special builds, such as companies wanting mobile displays, and this idea included motorhomes too. Chassis cab conversions were also built to special order by the company using lorry bases and all types of specials began to emerge from the Gosta Green Works. The company would also push its products at the Olympia show after its initial showing, while all the time adding to its range. With new owners of the Eccles caravans, it seemed that

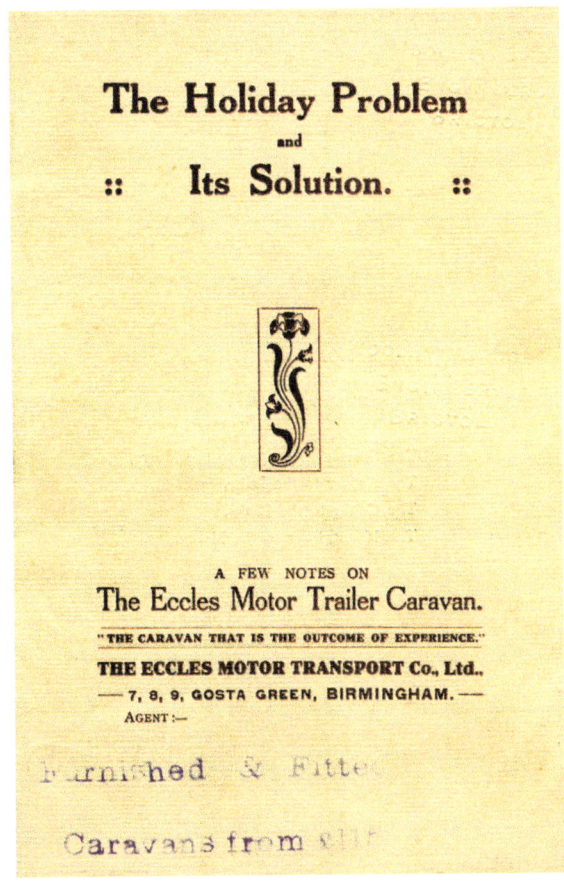

The idea of caravanning and motorhomes had to be marketed by the Riley team, so their slogan was 'The Holiday Problem & Its Solution'.

they would travel all over the world, writing back to the factory about how good the experience was. Newspaper reports told of how caravanning was growing increasingly popular and soon the middle classes would also be able to afford a caravan, making it a hobby for a wider audience.

Around 1924, the 9 ft Eccles with rear back end platform.

2137

Messrs Woolley Bros., Ltd., Date June 25th 1923.

61, St Georges Rd.,

Bristol.

DR. to

TELEPHONE No. CENTRAL 472.

WE SELL ALL MAKES OF CARS.

ECCLES MOTOR TRANSPORT LTD.

AUTOMOBILE ENGINEERS,

7, 8 & 9, GOSTA GREEN.

BIRMINGHAM.

Wm. Turner.

To one Eccles Family Trailer Caravan, list price	£155.	0s	0d
less 15% discount	23.	5s	0d
	£131.	15s	0d

7, 8 & 9, GOSTA GREEN.

684 BIRMINGHAM. June 25th 1923.

Received of Messrs Woolley Bros., Ltd.,

on Account of

Eccles Motor Transport, Ltd.

the sum of One Hundred and Thirty One Pounds Fifteen Shillings --- ------ --- ------

ECCLES MOTOR TRANSPORT LTD

£131.-.15s.-.-0d

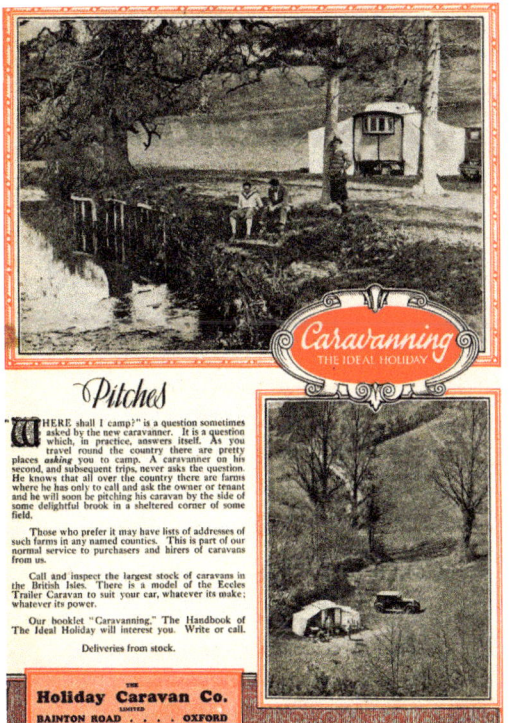

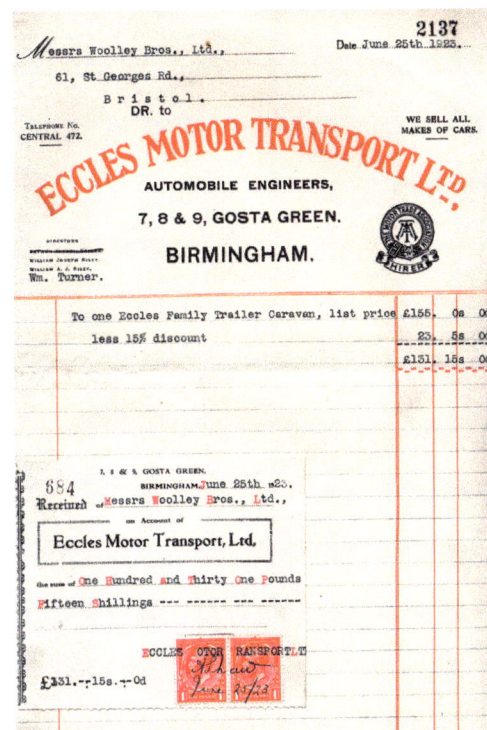

Above left: The Oxford Holiday Caravan Company hired and sold Eccles in the early days.

Above right: A 1923 rare invoice for an Eccles Caravan at £155, pre-discount!

Right: Woolley Bros of Bristol hired and sold Eccles caravans, as this booklet explained to potential owners, published around 1927.

ECCLES in the WEST

CARAVANS for HIRE

CONDITIONS AND PRICES.

WOOLLEY BROTHERS, 61, St. George's Road, College Green, BRISTOL.

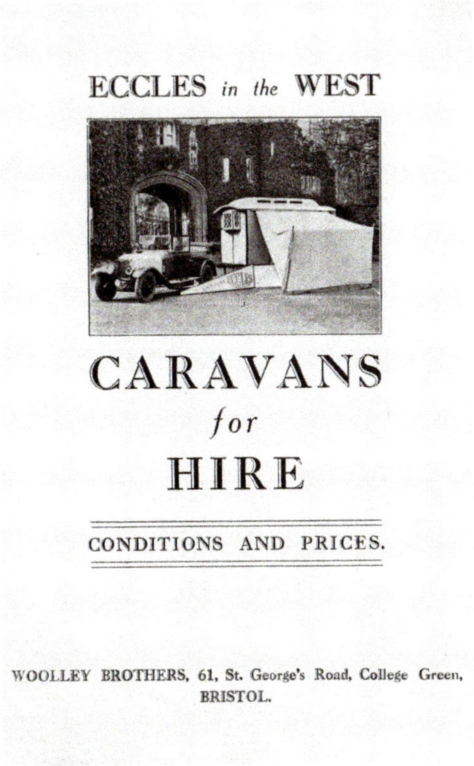

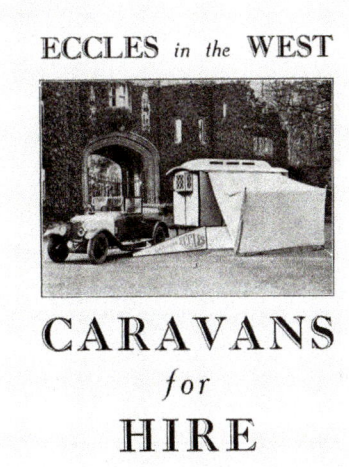

Eccles were producing specials such as this superb outfit in the early '20s.

Left: Another special outside the Eccles Gosta Green works after they had been renovated.

Below: The London Caravan Company was a first Eccles dealer; the photo was one of many sent from this customer on a long tour of 7,000 miles.

ALL ROUND EUROPE — One of a large batch of photographs sent to the London Caravan Company by a customer of theirs who has completed a tour of over 7,000 miles with this imposing Eccles outfit. It is seen here in Barcelona.

THE CARAVAN HOLIDAY
A Fortnight's Family Holiday for Just Over £4 Per Head

A picturesque camping site alongside a lily-covered pool. The caravan is an Eccles, and extra accommodation is provided by a lean-to.

Newspapers were contacted to help publicise how good value caravanning was – £4 a head! Note the 'lean-to tent' for added space.

Newspapers reported in 1925 that touring caravans were to be seen on warm sunny days in greater numbers – they were Eccles of course!

Autocar & Motor Magazine published several articles by Eccles owners who wrote about their experience owning the Eccles caravan and how wonderful the caravan life was, sending in pictures of their Eccles pitched up in some idyllic location in the UK. The romantic idea of pitching where you wanted and with little care for time saw caravanning being further promoted. Newspapers would take great PR shots using Eccles caravans as their setting, usually with 'young things' in the shot to show how fashionable caravanning was. Caravanning was beginning to take off as the 1920s progressed – no doubt helped by these great PR shots.

With hiring now becoming a popular way of getting the eventual sale of an Eccles caravan, a series of models were now available, though most of these would get an alteration in some way as the customer demanded. The Eccles would have screw-down corner steadies but the company would also fit overrun brakes as modern touring caravans. It was either this system or use a separate lever on the car to apply the caravan brakes.

Eccles owners enjoying a delightful pitch – these images added appeal to the caravanning ideals.

Another PR picture of two Eccles tourers; owners sent them to *Motor & Autocar Magazine,* which willingly published such images.

1930 and the girls are set up to show caravanning is healthy and fun.

Shots like this made even washing-up fun!

The overrun system was used by many Eccles owners but the South Devon town of Honiton had seen its police force 'pull' Eccles owners for not having a separate handbrake. Riley Junior was dispatched to Honiton to fight the Eccles owners' case. It was 1927 and with a new solicitor Riley had the right backing; after a lengthy hearing plus a practical trial, the case was thrown out. Innovative Eccles thinking saw this type of braking get legal approval a decade later.

With Eccles being the pioneer of car-pulled caravans and motorhomes, it was inevitable that other new manufacturers would begin to creep in. Makers such as Car Cruiser, Raven, Winchester and Cheltenham would appear, developing their slant on what a car-pulled caravan should look like. It also helped further highlight caravanning and Eccles gained more sales in the process. The transport side of the business was to be sold off as the caravan side grew, as did the motorhome section. More motorhomes were being ordered for both private and commercial use.

Eccles would further develop the motorhome side, making it a far front leader in this side of the business. It would also pursue caravans for living in either on a plot of land or on holiday, making them unaware producers of the first static caravan! By 1925 the original works was less suited to any major upgrade in output. Land at Stirchley, consisting of over 4.5 acres, was purchased with a new production plant being built especially for caravans to be manufactured. By 1928 the new factory was again further extended as sales increased, and by 1934 stock of over £25,000 was held along with a payroll of over £300 a week.

With a new dust-proof paint shop and new machinery operated by electric power, the plant was thus designed to make production smoother. The latest wood-working machinery was employed, making Eccles leaders in caravan and motorhome production. Camping trailers, telescopic caravans, touring caravans, horse box trailers, horse-drawn specials, motorhomes, trailers and even fifth-wheelers were built at the Eccles works. Super luxury 'living vans', designed with separate compartments and having four wheels, were built for showmen and Gypsies to travel in style.

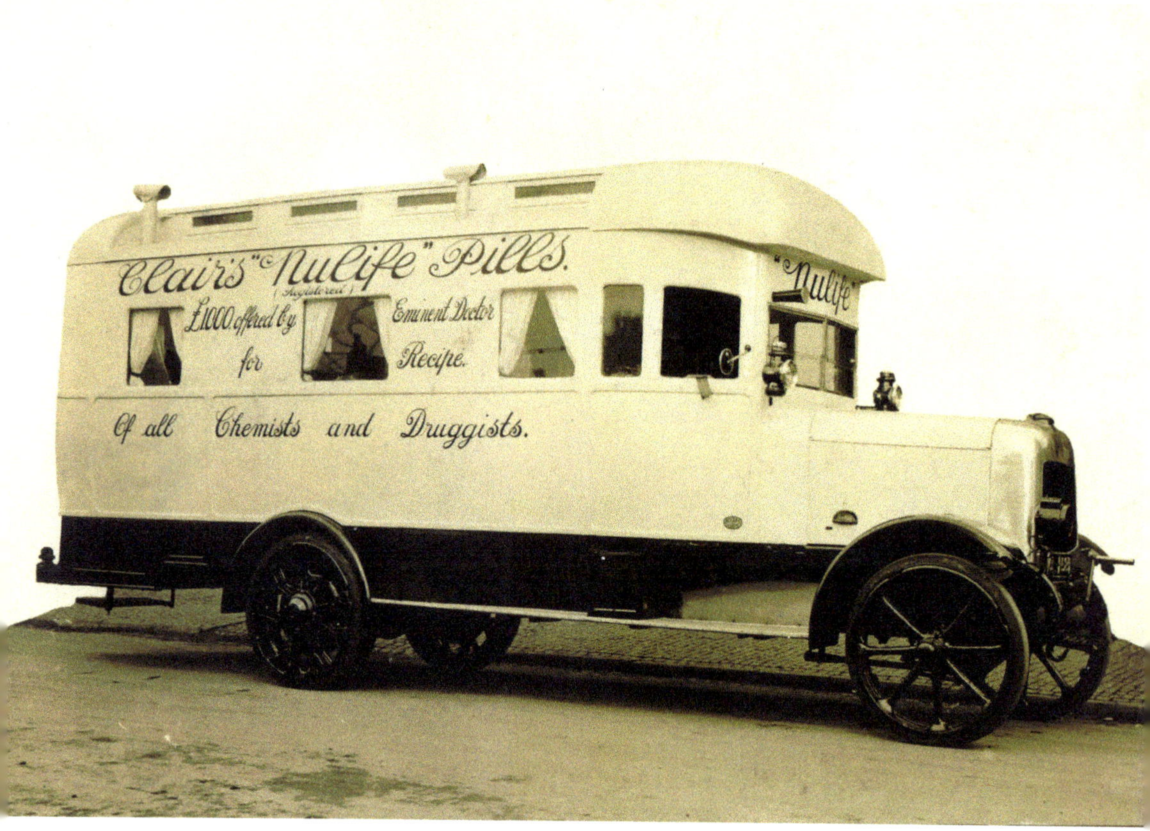

Special Eccles AEC-based motorhome (1923) for a family who also made and sold 'well-being' pills, which were dispensed on their travels!

A plan view of the interior of the home and business caravan, which has been provided with every comfort and all necessary facilities for a pill-maker's business.

B35

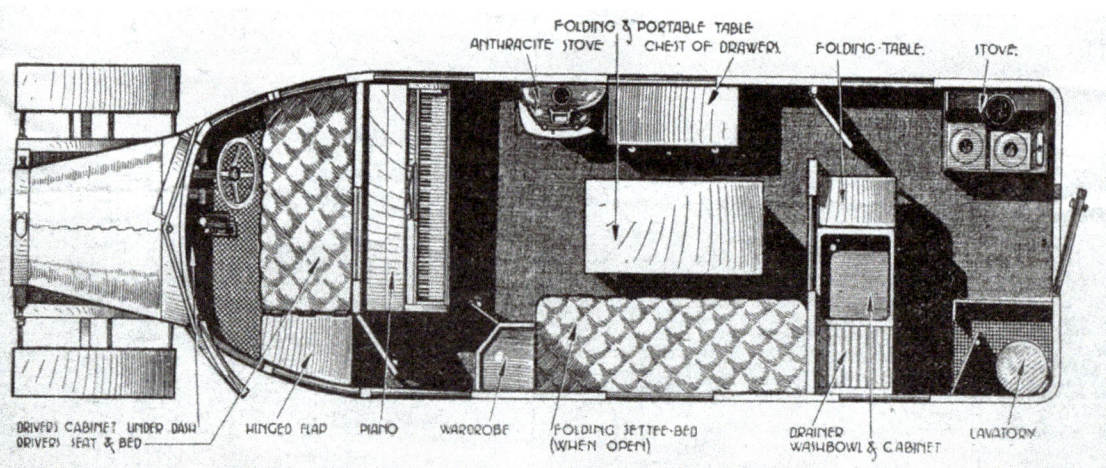

Exploded shot of the special – just what you needed if you had a pill-making business!

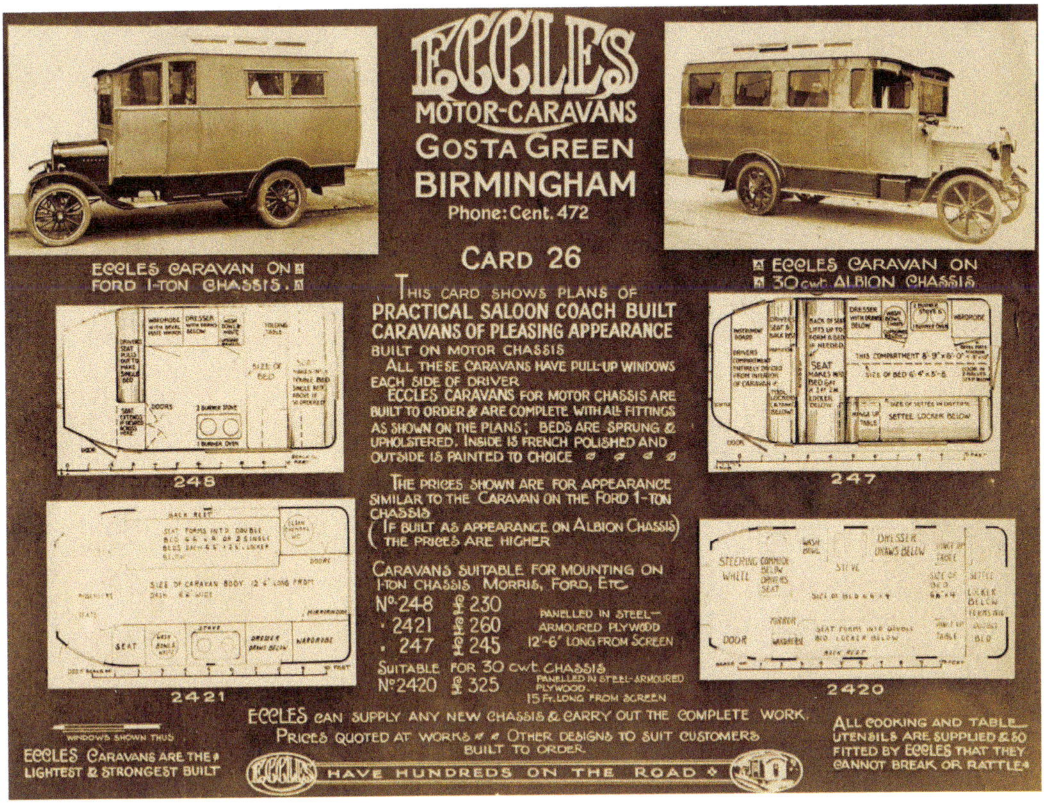

Motorhomes were a strong sector of the Eccles business in the early days, as these two models show.

Six-wheeler motorhome from the early 1920s – probably another customer special order. Eccles were ahead of the game with this leisure vehicle.

The Stirchley Eccles works in 1927 with staged caravans and a motorhome coming out of the factory door.

1926; a plain Eccles design of 14 ft length with two ladies drinking tea.

Another special, a fifth-wheeler from 1928 made for a US customer.

Eccles' skilled craftsmen could build all types of specials.

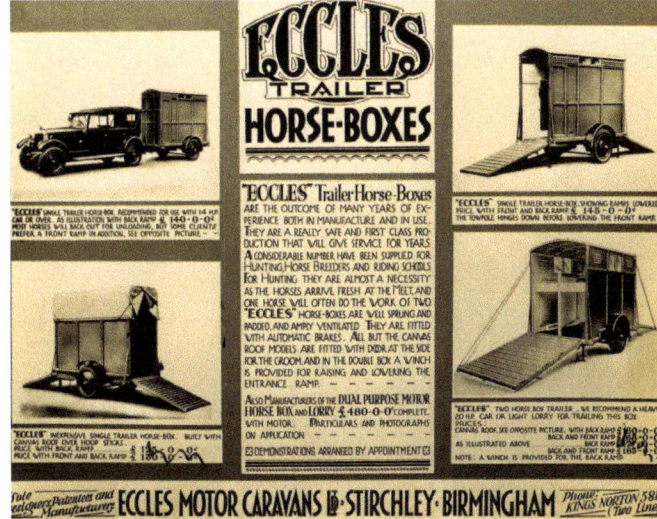

The company also built trailers and trailer horse boxes for a while in the 1920s.

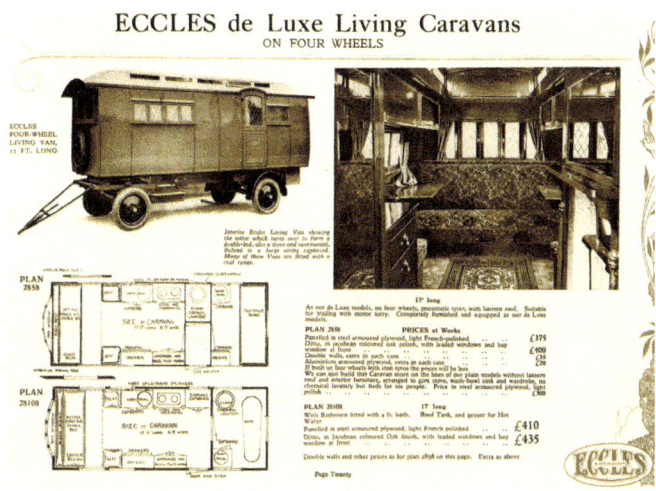

Typical luxury living van designed for showmen with ornate fittings – an Eccles speciality.

Eccles was becoming known as the best and word travelled, with many of the Eccles models being sent abroad. Many users testified to the Eccles being the most practical caravan in design and construction. Even royalty from abroad also bought an Eccles, among various other organisations. Film stars such as Gracie Fields and Nora Swinburne would take to the Eccles and caravanning. Eccles further gained a high profile from these sales to the famous, keeping the brand as prolific as ever. Back in 1928, famed American author Sinclair Lewis with his new bride Dorothy Thompson honeymooned in the UK with their special Eccles four-wheeler, adding to the prestigious line-up of Eccles owners. In 1929, Lord Baden Powell was presented with a 9 ft lantern-roofed Eccles by the Scout movement – this caravan still exists in 2017!

Our Gracie! Big star Gracie Fields owned an Eccles and helped publicise this fact.

Nora Swinburne, film star, at the window of her newly purchased Eccles at the Motor Show.

American author Sinclair Lewis spent his honeymoon travelling the UK with his Eccles.

With national press coverage too, Eccles was always the chosen models as the hobby took on further popularity. Described as ideal for health and getting fresh air, the Eccles was now a successful caravan brand. The company would also push for a new caravan towing speed limit. Eccles managed to persuade the powers that be that the 20 mph limit should be increased to 30 mph. Riley Junior fought for the change and by the early '30s the towing limit was increased. In 1932 Mr Riley Senior became ill and passed away, leaving Riley Junior Chairman and MD, with his brother – H. A. Riley, a chartered accountant – also joining the board. Meetings were held with dealers and after eighteen months sales were climbing higher than ever.

The '30s would see a new breed of Eccles; the age of streamlining had begun and the rather square designs harking back to horse-drawn caravans were to give way to new aerodynamic designs. Winchester – Bertram Hutchings had in 1930 produced a very streamlined tourer. Eccles would work on their own designs and by 1932 they had moved away from the squarer look. Additionally, 1932 proved a success for the Eccles durability programme with an entry in the Monte Carlo Rally; the Eccles, towed by a Hillman Wizard, finished the gruelling rally. Riley himself was part of the crew and was always keen to trial his caravans as part of his design strategy. The next trial was a Sahara Desert trip with another Hillman car for this endurance run. With a team of four, led by MD of the Nomad

Caravan Company, Clive Scarff, they set off with an Eccles Nymphette, travelling thousands of miles through Africa and other continents, going where no caravan had been before! The trip was a big success and earned more sales for Eccles abroad. The Eccles used on the trip became affectionately known as the Nomad Arms!

At the first caravan rally held at Minehead in 1933, the Eccles was the most popular make and also picked up several prizes for design. He would take several weeks before he made the decision to build it. This he did with the new-look Eccles, starting with the new lightweight Ecclite range, which consisted of two models – one a 9 ft version and the other a 12 ft version. The design was still traditional by 1934, though the streamlined Eccles was beginning to hit the roads. In 1935 a small child's-type booklet told the story of a made-up family, written in rhyme with photos and illustrations describing their holidays.

By 1933, Eccles were more streamlined in design.

An Eccles Nymphette in the Sahara; nicknamed the Nomad Arms, this was a trip that covered thousands of miles with the Eccles staying intact.

22

 ROOMY LIGHTWEIGHT CARAVANS

Interior 9 ft. 6 ins. "ECCLITE," looking towards front.

9 ft. 6 ins. MODEL

"ECCLITE" TRAILER CARAVAN. A ROOMY, LIGHT-WEIGHT CARAVAN TO SLEEP THREE, AND EASILY TOWED WITH AN 8-10 H.P. CAR.

COMPLETELY FURNISHED **£105**

BRIEF SPECIFICATION.

SEATS. Both seats pull out flat to form single beds. Cushion across the end lifts up at night to form a bunk bed. All beds and seats are comfortably sprung and upholstered in tasteful materials, with large locker below each seat.

STOVE. Double burner Valor Perfection Stove, with single oven, is provided in metal-lined recess. An excellent cooker.

DRESSER. This is similar to the dresser in the 12 ft. model. With washbowl and outlet, lid, and cupboard below. Above the dresser is a shelf with table and cooking utensils.

WARDROBE. Below the wardrobe is a further cupboard containing food safe.

ROOF LOCKERS. Shown where indicated on plan.

UNDERWORKS. Built on reinforced chassis with springs and greaser shackles, Timken roller bearings, detachable disc wheels, and Dunlop tyres, adjustable legs, towpole, with patent operation to the automatic internal expanding brakes.

PRICE. Completely equipped with table and cooking utensils in rattleproof devices, linoleum, curtains, painted Beige and lined Green as standard (or to choice) **£105.**

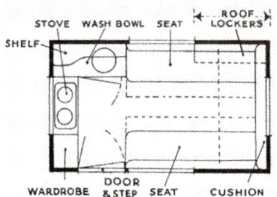

It is important to note that the whole of the sides and roofs of the "ECCLITE" Caravans are panelled in plywood. This plywood is again covered on the outside with canvas cemented down and well painted (seven coats). This preserves the plywood from damp and disintegration, and a solid built caravan of extraordinary low weight is thus provided, which gives proper protection and comfort to the occupants and will stand up to the use of many years.

Above: A lightweight Ecclite 9 ft caravan from 1929, costing £105 fully furnished.

Right: In 1935 Eccles published this little book of a made-up Eccles family.

23

Down winding lane both John and Jane,
　And likewise Jack and Jill,
Wend their way from day to day;
　Of fresh air drink their fill.
Beside the sea to stay they're free
　Or move on as they please.
They ramble, swim, grow lithe of limb,
　Or rest and take their ease.

In rain or shine the life is fine
　Because they're free to roam,
All tanned deep brown afar from town—
　Yet never far from home!
And so at last their fortnight's past
　With Jack and Jill all freckles:
The secret's—yes! we thought you'd guess—
　Their caravan's an ECCLES.

　　　　p.s.
The weekends, too, are their's, remember
From May right into warm September.

　So ends
　　　THE STORY PLAIN
　　　　　of JOHN and JANE—

✱✱✱
OF COURSE
John and Jane
chose an Eccles.

It contains all
the refinements
mentioned on the
previous pages,
and many more.

Be sure to get
the ECCLES full
catalogue—see
back page.

The little book was in rhyme and came well illustrated.

By 1933 another factory extension was added, making the premises a total of 36,000 sq ft. With all types of work being carried out, including the Gibson trailers and other engineering, Eccles were proving the largest producer of caravans and by 1936 four lines would be used for production. New models were being introduced that were more affordable and new luxury models were added too. Names such as Road Nymph, Enchantress, and Imperial would be joined in 1937 by other models. These included the mid-priced Regent, based on the 65 model but with lantern roof and double-panelled walls.

The luxury Aristocrat was designed for all-year use and the super luxury Senator at nearly 18 ft in length was also introduced. Radio, water tank, insulated walls and roof and 12-volt lighting all came in at £435. The cheapest 1937 model was the single wall panelled 65 model at £168. By 1938 the President and Independent, plus a new model – the 55 – were added. By 1939, with the Second World War looming, other areas were being explored but caravan production was running high with new profiles and replacement models being added. The Democrat was one for 1939, being an all-year-use tourer with an oil stove and 12-volt lighting. Eccles also launched its National, a caravan which could be more mass-produced and thus have the price lowered. It could be gas or oil-equipped, costing just £130. Made to a standard format, it sold well that year.

In late 1938, the Eccles Owners Club was formed, with an annual dinner held the following December and a first rally in May 1939. The Club would cease, but was then reformed in 1969. Eccles had also been forward-thinking in opening a London showroom, which would shut at the outbreak of war.

The Showroom was opened in November 1938 at 379 Heddon Way, north-west London. It was attended by trade and private caravanners and a luncheon was supplied. It was seen as an important step of raising the profile of caravans in general, but mainly of course to Eccles' advantage. It also gave the company prestige and, as well as the caravans, the Gibson trailers were also displayed too.

However, with the onset of the Second World War it began to look bleak for Eccles, with caravan work drying up. This resulted in Riley going out in search of other work for the recently extended factory, which will be looked at in the next chapter as we see how Eccles survived the Second World War after a very successful last decade building up dealers across the UK.

Above: Eccles' works being extended to increase production in the mid-30s.

Right: The trailer side of Eccles, named Gibson, was for some time a lucrative part of the business, especially in the 1930s.

25

The Eccles Road Nymph was launched in 1935 and was designed for all-year use.

F. M. L. Harris, the editor of *The Caravan*, had an Eccles costing £425 designed especially for him, naming it *Liberty Hall IV* in 1936.

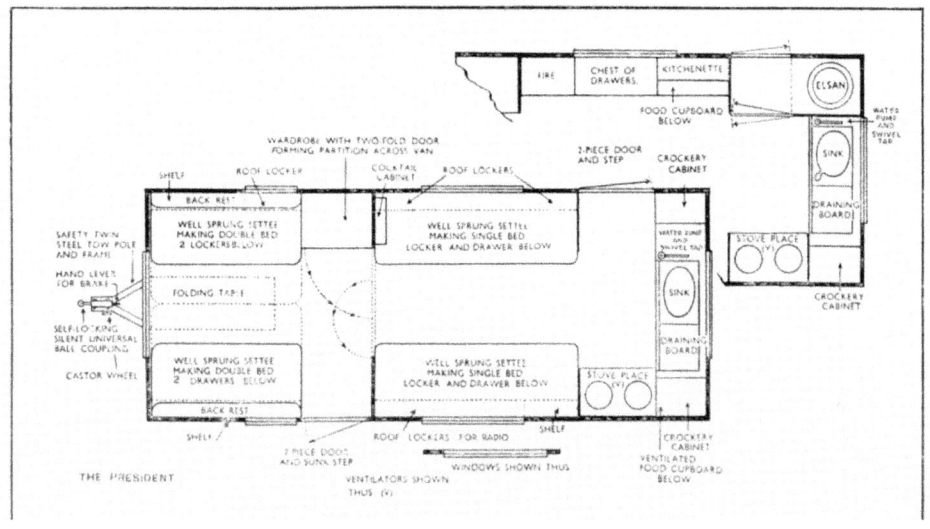

Interior of Eccles "President."
A Place for everything and everything in its place.

The Eccles President from 1939 had two layout options.

The *Eccles "Democrat"*

The 1939 Democrat had a lowered floor, as did other 1939 Eccles models, to add more headroom. Towing stability was also improved.

The luxury Eccles Senator from 1938 was a luxury tourer, and if ordered with gas and gas fridge cost £465.

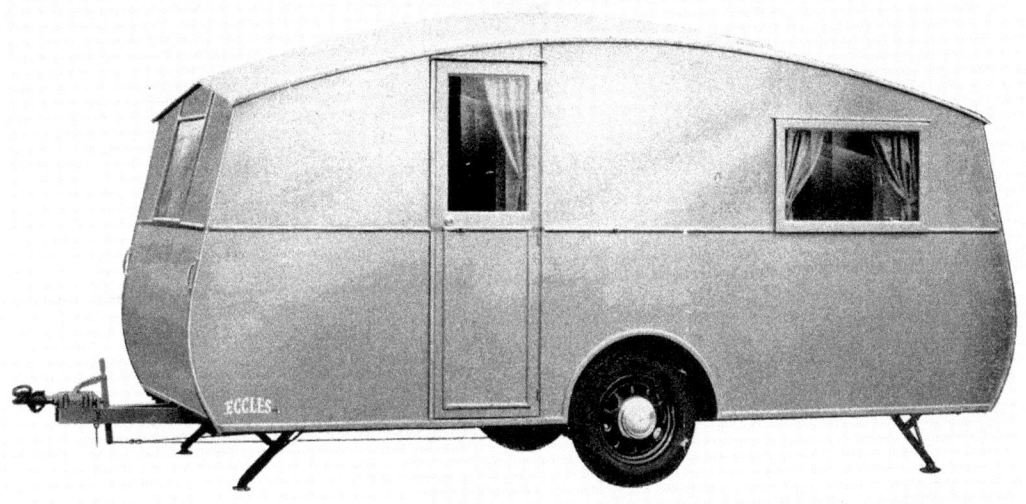

- Size 14' 6" x 6' 6"
- Two rooms, separated by partition from floor to ceiling.
- Pullman double bed and two single beds, to sleep 4 persons.
- Double-panelled walls and ceiling insulate against extremes of temperature.
- Generous food storage accommodation.

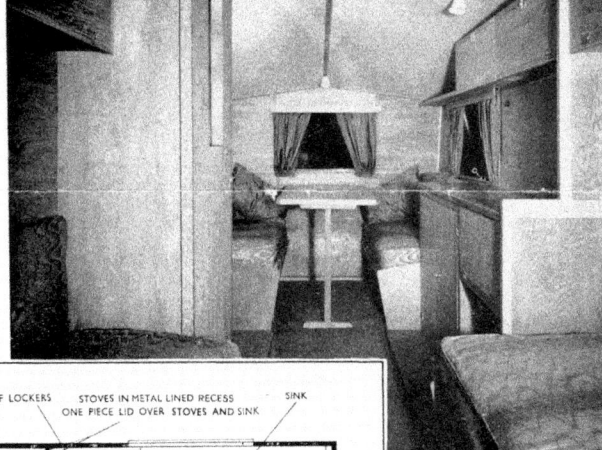

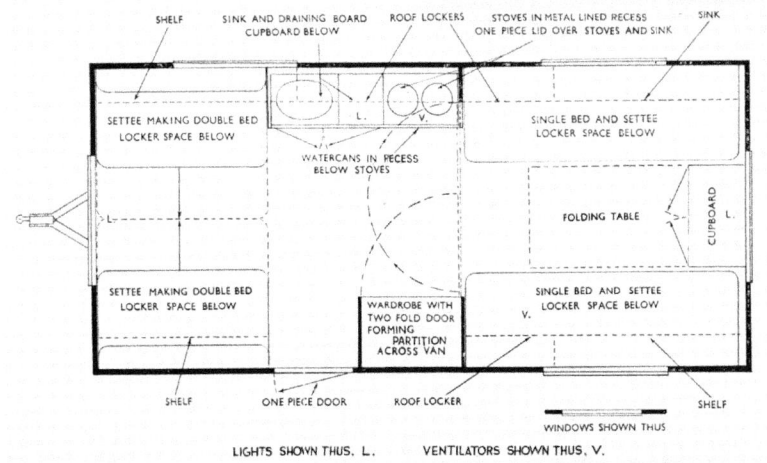

The 'National' has been skilfully planned for the utmost comfort and utility. The double panelled walls and ceiling maintain even temperature, and the large metal-lined ventilated food cupboard keeps foodstuffs fresh and sweet. These are important features.

London Showrooms : 379, HENDON WAY, HENDON, N.W.4
Telephone : HENdon 3355

The Eccles National from 1939 proved a sales success, although it was only produced for a year.

29

Eccles' swish showrooms at 379 Heddon Way, north-west London, in 1938 on the opening day of business.

Woolley Bros of Bristol's mid-1930s showroom was an early Eccles dealership.

Chapter Two

Eccles Develops New Models and Lead in Caravan Mass Production

The Rileys had been aware that another war was brewing up, and it was no secret that Riley had approached various government departments regarding work that could be carried out in engineering and other coachbuilding at the Eccles works as far back as 1936! Eccles had spent over £4,000 on further building work, including air raid shelters, so they needed some return quick! Plans had been put forward for 'in the field' mobile offices but the Ministry of Defence declined the prototype, while the Germans actually used such units on the battlefield. In fact, the mobile HQs the War Office had turned down in 1937 now became a firm order of forty! But it wasn't long before the Eccles design, quality and productivity

Riley had built this special mobile army HQ in 1937; the War Office took over two years to order forty of them!

was seen as beneficial to war work and the factory was put into full production making mobile searchlights, ambulances, trailers, fire tenders and laboratories. More steel work was called for and this saw new skills at the Eccles works. In pre-war days the company had looked at steel frames for caravan construction. This had witnessed new machines that were ideal for the new work coming in. Orders flooded in and the wages bill also climbed. With little cash left in the bank account, the company hit the red for the first time in years. War work was flowing but the money was slow to follow and Eccles was on the verge of going bust. The bank stuck with the company and disaster was averted.

The war years were hard and though a few caravans were built, the next five years were spent learning a great deal about production methods and turning out war work. Eccles had been advanced pre-war, with sectional-made furniture and mass-production introduced specially for the 1939 National caravan. Some work came with technical problems but Eccles overcame such difficulties. Other caravan manufacturers were also doing war work but Eccles led the field. After the war some caravan manufacturers never returned, while other new concerns began to shoot up.

By mid-1945, with the war over and no more orders, it was seen that the factory had to look elsewhere. Luckily, the steel section side of the business was ahead, getting back to new products such as steel trucks, and stillages, among other steel products. With war work carried out by Eccles, they managed to get certain materials and machinery to develop new products from steel. The caravan side of the business had to be built back up and 300 vans were to be constructed, but of only one design.

Quite basic (by pre-war Eccles standards) but with new production methods of numbered jigs and efficient castings, the new model – named the Enterprise – was also sold as a 'home' to help the housing shortage. A number were sold to the US forces at Burtonwood in the North West to help with accommodation. The price was good at £534 or £564, with gas lights and a stove, in 1946/7. It was built using flow-line production and was a basic solid design to serve a purpose rather than being fitted with gimmicks.

With the engineering side kept separate, the caravan side was the back-up. Caravans would be produced in batches and specials almost stopped, though the company was doing well with exports. Pensions and apprentices were brought into the Eccles organisation and new models were being designed, especially as now a new breed of manufacturers had evolved after 1946. Caravans were more affordable and the luxury makers such as Winchester would fold at the end of the 1950s.

Eccles would follow on from the success of the Enterprise with models such as the larger £715 Progress in 1949, and the Alert – also launched in 1949 – was to prove a massive success with five years in production and over 1,500 units sold! The Alert would see successful sales in Europe, with France being a particularly good customer, while Northern Rhodesia and even Arabia helped boost sales further. The Active was a lower-priced family 13 ft Eccles model at £348 and was another post-war model introduced for 1949.

In 1951 the Eccles Advance sported the idea of a flexible seating arrangement, allowing the seats to be free-standing and moved outside in summer! But the Advance only lasted one season, being replaced by the Adventure luxury model for 1952, which sported an 18 ft x 7 ft layout, the first such since the war. It came with an ingenious drop-down-side double bed, designed by Eccles, who also patented it. Designed as a 'living mobile home', its construction

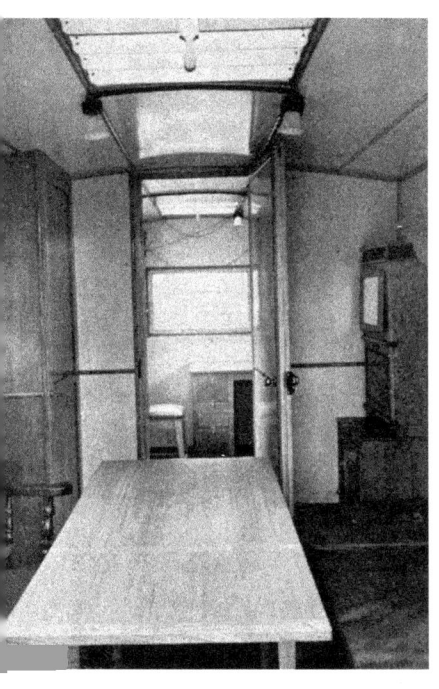

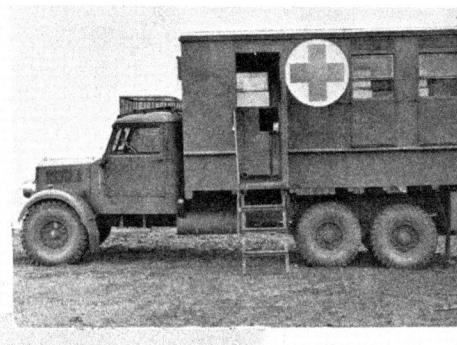

BODIES BY ECCLES

A dental laboratory on Ford chassis.

Searchlight vehicle on Tilling-Stevens chassis.

29

Above left: Interior of the special war unit with sleeping accommodation and a small office – Riley, a man of ideas, was at it again!

Above right: The Eccles plant was kept busy during the war, turning out a full array of vehicles helped by their modern machinery and skilled workforce.

Below left: Heavy-duty vehicles were built to do all sorts of war work.

Below right: Advert describing Eccles' war work in 1942.

AT the present time we are fully occupied on important work in large quantities. We are convinced that the experience gained, during wartime, in large scale production will enable us to bring to our customers better value and improved designs.

With pride we look back on our past achievements, and we look forward with confidence to the time when we shall be able to offer the great British Public

The **BEST VALUE** *in* **CARAVAN**!

ECCLES

ECCLES, (BIRMINGHAM) LTD.,
STIRCHLEY, BIRMINGHAM, 30.

33

ECCLES' STEEL PRODUCTS

1.—GENERAL PURPOSE TRUCK. The open sides facilitate the loading and unloading of boxes, small sacks, etc.
2.—SACK TRUCK. Suitable for handling bales or large sacks.
3.—TRUCK ON CASTOR WHEELS. Suitable for general use, and specially suitable for use on wood floors.
4.—GENERAL PURPOSE TRUCK. Suitable for warehouse and general use.

Above left: Experience in engineering saw a surge in new steel products after the war at Stirchley.

Above right: The interior of the Enterprise lacked the luxury of Eccles of old; a new age had begun in value, quality caravans from Eccles.

racked up a hefty weight of over 30 cwt. However, the caravan press said the £850 Adventure, with its high specification, would be a good touring caravan for families too.

The 1950s would see some of the old model names come back, such as Democrat, Aristocrat and Imperial. Eccles had always been public show exhibitors right from the word go and continued at Earls Court after the war; the company would exhibit cut-away models, such as of the Alert and the Coronation, letting the public see just how well-made and designed Eccles caravans were. In fact, the Alert had taken eight months to develop before production began, with many ideas and problems having to be ironed out.

Eccles designers discussed what they wanted and then the design was actually built, pre-drawings! Eccles called their system building 'live' so an actual prototype was built that was then tested for weight and towing stability. Jack Robinson, an 'old hand' at Eccles and a mainstay of the factory, was involved with design and production of the Alert. Very much an Eccles man, he had started in 1934 with the company as a buyer. He would later leave Eccles before the Sprite buyout in 1960.

Eccles was producing quality caravans and at a good price with their highly efficient factory. Each year they brought out new models or updated an existing model, usually with an 'MK' suffix at the end. Upper-priced models were also joined by mid-priced tourers such as the Bounty – another popular model in the mid to late '50s – but also the E series, which

Above left: At the end of 1945 the Eccles Enterprise is in production, being mass-produced with techniques learnt from war work.

Above right: The Enterprise sold well and got Eccles back into the industry from 1946.

was designed for export but was also sold to UK buyers. The E series was simpler in design and thus cheaper to build, which kept prices down.

Chassis were still designed and built by Eccles, ensuring correct and accurate fixings for the various bodyshells. Laminate timber was used for the main bodywork which was often from off-cuts but useable for construction. From 1954 the Birmingham plant could average around 1,500 caravans a year, which covered all the model lengths up to 20 ft. The Eccles design team were always wanting feedback and this was encouraged, especially with the old Caravan Club members who often unwittingly influenced the Eccles design team. At the end of 1954, Eccles purchased 12.5 acres of land at Redditch, 10 miles from the Stirchley plant; the only problem was that labour was in short demand, but the Rileys were prepared to bus workers to the new plant once it was in operation.

Although Eccles had indeed cut back on specials (due to them being unprofitable), they would adapt a standard model into various special units such as the Eccles used to go on a trip to South America. The Eccles not only hadn't leaked, but it had been able to float across rivers too! The caravan was tested for such events and was found to be up to the job; typical of Eccles to also prove how durable their tourers were. Specials were fewer as time went on, the last being in 1960.

The Eccles factory could run four different models with its production system, though the Rileys feared too much production and the quality could slip. Models such as the larger Enchantress costing £675 and the Eversure Traveller at £875 were produced in 1959. It was in this period that along with Bluebird Caravans, Eccles didn't rejoin the National Caravan Council. The NCC didn't want NCC dealers/manufacturers to trade with non-members but Eccles and Bluebird did. The upshot was that the NCC allowed mutual trading and the two big makers rejoined.

A warranty was issued with each van built plus a small fold-out heavy-duty paper 'owner's manual' of sorts. The manual was basic but informative for the period. Eccles boasted

Above left: The Eccles team in 1946 – many had been with the company for over twenty years.

Above right: Eccles 1955 French brochure; export markets had always been key right from the early 1920s.

Export Alerts ready for dispatch to Northern Rhodesia.

1949 Eccles Progress models – a batch of three destined for Arabia.

36

The Eccles Active from 1949 was another new Eccles development.

The Alert interior was practical and functional and sold well.

The Eccles Advance from 1951 with the 'flexible' lounge seating that could be moved around.

37

Above left: The Eccles Adventure from 1952 was aimed at the upper end of the market.

Above right: The Eccles Aristocrat Mk2 from 1956 was also classed as a living van for travellers.

Showing exterior of the Eccles "New Imperial" caravan **18'** long, **7'** wide. Good headroom through

The Eccles New Imperial, launched for 1953, cost £460 and replaced the Adventure.

38

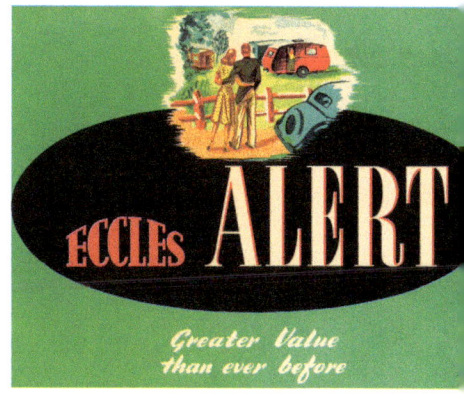

Above left: The Eccles Alert cut-away was used at many of the shows and the company also used this idea for the Coronation model in 1953.

Above right: The Alert was a new-look Eccles from 1949 which proved a top seller.

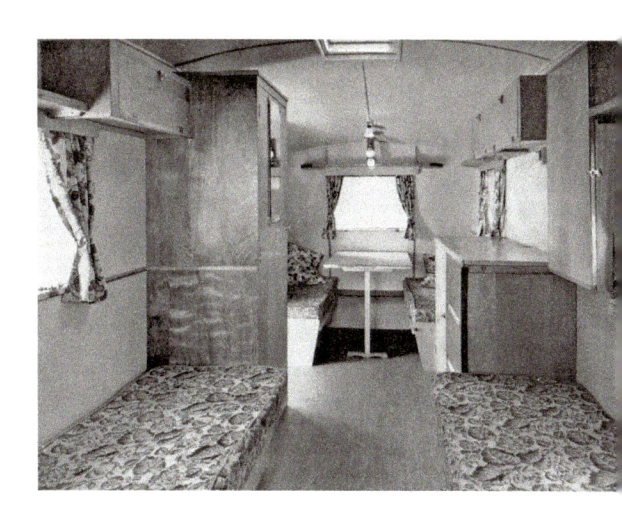

Interior of the Alert looking forward – note no backrests were fitted!

that very few owners ever needed warranty work, proving quality was key with Eccles. A breakdown of models in production was published by Eccles in the early '60s. The 12 ft Coronation, for instance, had 300 units sold in one season, while the 16 ft Democrat launched for 1954 sold 600 units into late 1955 with the Mk2 version. From the 1950s, Eccles' success abroad also saw sales doing well, with 5 to 15 per cent of output going for exports. The E series was made for this market but the E10 proved especially popular abroad.

Eccles was indeed a large company, though the new makes such as Paladin, Berkeley, Bluebird, Sprite and Willerby were making inroads in the market, thus making competition stiffer generally. Eccles' policy to always stock plenty of spares at the factory so that waiting times were kept low would ensure continued sales after the war. The company carried parts for pre-war models too, with the factory holding records of caravans from the beginning in 1919 as a record of what they had built.

Mr. W. J. Riley (seated), Mr. J. H. Robinson (centre) and Mr. H. West discuss the interior design of a model shown on a sketch prepared from the prototype.

Eccles' design still involved Bill Riley, who is pictured sat down as he discusses a new model for production.

The Bounty interior was pleasing and appealed to various export markets too.

The Eccles Bounty from 1955 proved a good seller and a year or two later also had a toilet room added at the front corner.

Eccles were seeing in the 1950s with good strong sales; the war had given the company valuable experience which they would utilise as much as possible with the caravans. The early '50s had seen such models as the Adventure and Advance and the celebratory Coronation in 1953 – a 12 ft four-berth built to a lighter weight for the smaller car owner that, as mentioned, sold well for Eccles. The Coronet in 1954, another small family tourer, would also see many sold over two years.

The stars of the period continued to see Eccles as an ideal caravan to fit their needs while on tour. That one-time saucy music hall comedian Max Miller purchased an Eccles in 1954 for touring the theatres. In 1953 the Birmingham mayor and mayoress were shown around the Eccles factory and were taken by how efficient the factory was – a credit to the Eccles team.

Eccles dealer Crabtree Caravans in Cheshire (no longer in business) took a 1955 Eccles Bounty on a continental tour with a Vauxhall Cresta tow car, both in matching colours of red and white. The Eccles was fitted with some special features and was dispatched to spread the word on caravanning Eccles style! When the British Caravan Road Rally began in the mid-50s, Eccles was a firm competitor and would be very prolific in the next decade. Eccles would flirt with specials manufacturer Coventry Steel Caravans. The year was 1953 and a joint venture witnessed Eccles build the van while Coventry Steel did the design. Named the Imperial Knight, it was set for the luxury market, costing £595 and coming well-equipped, including for mains electrics. The idea of a joint venture though was short lived.

The days of luxury caravans and specials were mainly over for Eccles and simpler and easier production was key in the firm's success. Competition was mounting and

Special Eccles Coronet built for a South American trip, which had to be able to float too!

Left: In 1959 the Eccles Enchantress made its appearance, but for that year only.

Below: The Eversure MkIV from 1958 was designed as a 'living' caravan or large tourer.

ENCHANTRESS

you'll be *MORE* at home in an **ECCLES**

Streamlined Production guided by the most experienced brains in the caravan world has produced this 19ft. living-touring caravan at an exceedingly moderate price. Luxurious to look at, luxurious to live in, the "Eversure" is indeed a caravan for those who want the very best. Many of the modifications and improvements of this model are the outcome of the ever welcome co-operation of Eccles owners. They may be sure that appreciation of their support will be reflected in yet greater achievements for their pleasure and satisfaction.

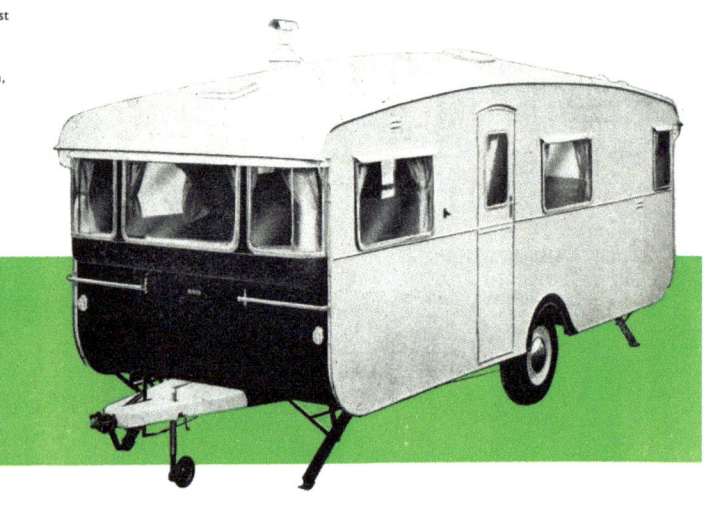

EVERSURE MK IV

models such as the Avenger, Nipper, and Landfarer were designed to compete with a new breed of caravans. Eccles hadn't done anything radical apart from production methods, and with Bill Riley's son tragically dead, the firm was in need of new blood to carry it into the next decade.

The next part of the Eccles story will see how the brand was re-invented and how it became part of the world's largest caravan manufacturing group with a new 'boss' at the helm.

Eccles (Birmingham) Limited.

**HAZELWELL LANE,
STIRCHLEY, BIRMINGHAM 30**

Guarantee No... Serial No...

Date of Purchase.. Type of Caravan...

Name and Address of Purchaser...

.... Date left Works..

SPECIMEN GUARANTEE

THIS IS TO CERTIFY that the above Caravan has been made in the factory of Eccles (Birmingham) Ltd., Stirchley, Birmingham (hereinafter termed " Eccles ") and, subject to the following Terms and Conditions, is guaranteed against defects due to faulty workmanship by Eccles and/or the use by Eccles of unreasonable material.

TERMS AND CONDITIONS

1. This Guarantee will expire on the earliest of the following dates :—
   The date being 9 months following that of purchase by the above named purchaser.
   That date being 12 months after the caravan left Eccles' Works.
   The date on which the Caravan ceases to be the property of the above named purchaser.

2. The Caravan (with the Serial Number therein intact for the purpose of identification) or the faulty part or parts, must be returned clearly labelled with the Sender's Name and Address, and the above Guarantee Number to Eccles' Works.

3. In the event of a part or parts being returned, and not the whole Caravan, the cost of refitting same shall be borne by the owner.

4. Eccles shall not be responsible for the payment of any freight, carriage or other cost in transit or Customs Duties which may be involved or which may be payable in respect of any Caravan, part or parts sent in exchange or repaired, all of which shall be paid by the owner.

5. This Guarantee shall not apply to any Caravan which shall have been altered or repaired outside Eccles' Works so as, in Eccles' opinion, to affect its road-worthiness, reliability or weatherproofness nor to any Caravan which has been hired out or subjected to misuse, accident or insufficient maintenance. (NOTE : A Maintenance Schedule is supplied with each Caravan).

6. This Guarantee does not apply to paintwork, as the affects of climatic conditions and periods of exposure are incalculable.

7. This Guarantee does not apply to tyres, wheels, stoves or other fittings or apparatus not manufactured by Eccles, but Eccles, if asked, will render what assistance they can to obtain satisfaction, and give the names of makers.

8. This Guarantee is operative only in favour of the Purchaser named above and shall not be assignable and no warranty or guarantee is given to or shall be implied in favour of any other person or persons.

9. The decision of Eccles on any question arising out of this Guarantee shall be accepted as final and binding.

Purchasers of Eccles Caravans and products shall be deemed to purchase the same after full inspection and approval, subject to and with the benefit of this guarantee, and all other conditions, guarantees, representations and warranties whether expressed or implied and which might exist but for this provision, and every liability (if any) for consequential damage by reason of any defect latent or otherwise are hereby expressly excluded, and Eccles neither assume nor authorize any other person to assume for them any other liability in connection with the sale of Eccles Caravans and products.

You have received and entered into a Contract incorporating Eccles Terms of Business and this Guarantee given to you by them is deemed to be part of that Contract.

Dated this..day of..19..........

For and on behalf of ECCLES (BIRMINGHAM) LIMITED.

Director..

The Eccles guarantee – it was said few owners ever needed to use it, such was the quality of Eccles caravans.

1st Aug.

You should Read this —

★ *it is important...*

INSTRUCTIONS FOR THE MAINTENANCE OF YOUR

ECCLES
CARAVAN

In all correspondence please quote the serial number which you will find on the metal plate inside the wardrobe and also on the left-hand main entrance door pillar. Remove paint to read the latter. We endeavour to keep constructional records of all Eccles Caravans and this serial number enables us to give immediate attention to your enquiry.

... on the left hand main entrance door pillar ...

ISSUED JUNE, 1953

The Eccles owner's manual from 1953 – a small booklet supplied with each new caravan.

E.10

SPECIFICATION

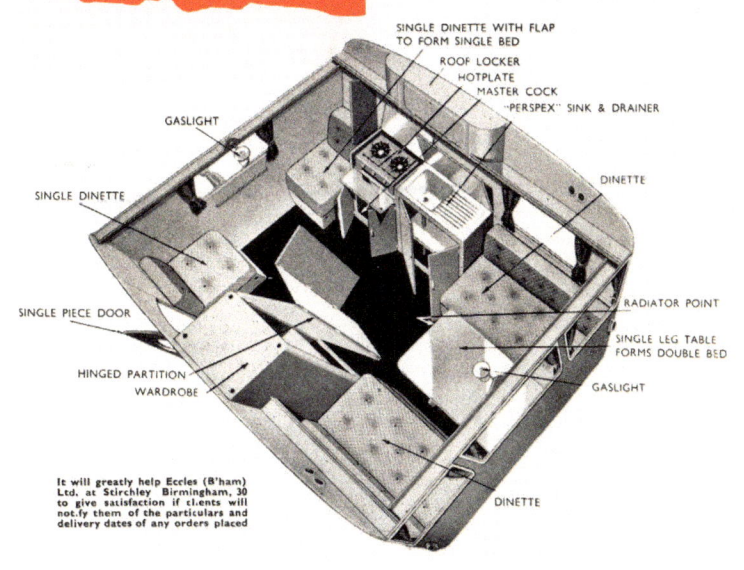

- SINGLE DINETTE WITH FLAP TO FORM SINGLE BED
- ROOF LOCKER
- HOTPLATE
- MASTER COCK
- "PERSPEX" SINK & DRAINER
- GASLIGHT
- SINGLE DINETTE
- DINETTE
- SINGLE PIECE DOOR
- RADIATOR POINT
- SINGLE LEG TABLE FORMS DOUBLE BED
- HINGED PARTITION
- WARDROBE
- GASLIGHT
- DINETTE

It will greatly help Eccles (B'ham) Ltd. at Stirchley Birmingham, 30 to give satisfaction if clients will notify them of the particulars and delivery dates of any orders placed

The E Series was honed for the export markets; the E10 was well-received for the 1957 season.

Introducing THE NEW ECCLES "CORONATION"

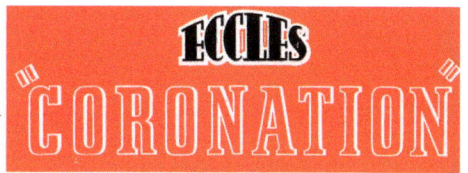

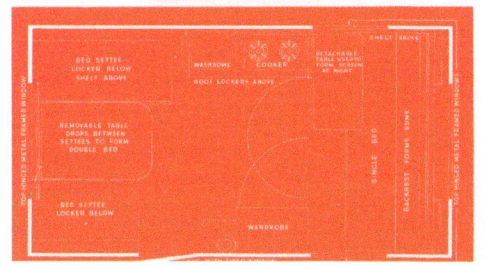

12 ft. LIGHTWEIGHT TOURING CARAVAN

For the Small Car Owner

The successful manufacture of the modern caravan depends largely on keeping abreast, and sometimes ahead, of current demands and trends. With the introduction of the "Coronation" Eccles provide striking evidence of their continual awareness of present day caravan requirements.

Whilst maintaining the standard and constructional quality with which the name Eccles dominates the Caravan world, extensive machine modernisation and consequent economical production has enabled the price factor to be given primary consideration. A long period of research, a considerable amount of foresight and a great deal of thought has gone into the production of this new model.

For 30 years the quality of Eccles Caravans has set the standard by which others are judged—but for suitability to modern requirements the "Coronation" is beyond comparison.

The Coronation was launched for 1953 to commemorate the Queen's coronation of that year; it sported the new V-line roof design.

45

The Coronation replacement, the Coronet, at a European show.

Cheeky Chappie star Max Miller bought a new Eccles Democrat; behind is Jack Robinson of Eccles.

The snapshots from the Mayor of Birmingham's visit to the Eccles works; bottom right, the mayoress (with cigarette in mouth!) chats to Bill Riley.

Crabtree Caravans, a Cheshire dealership, went on a continental trip with the Eccles Bounty and matching Vauxhall Cresta tow car in 1955.

An Eccles entrant in the British Caravan Road Rally.

COVENTRY STEEL'S NEW IMPERIAL KNIGHT

ENTERING the sphere of the more orthodox, Coventry Steel Caravans Ltd. announce the Imperial Knight—a combination of Eccles coachwork and Coventry Steel design. The 18 ft. 6 in. exterior shell is aluminium and the interior is hardboard, the cavity insulated with glass wool. The chassis is Eccles-built, with a Brockhouse coupling. The interior layout is based on a rear end kitchen, with a double dinette forward and a settee/double bed amidships. In the rear offside corner is a toilet compartment. Fitted for mains electricity, with solid fuel stove and hot-water tank, the Imperial Knight costs £595.

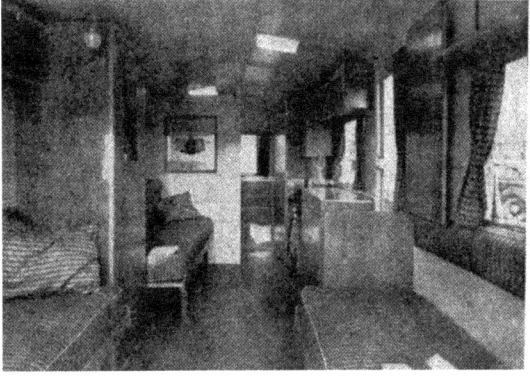

Coventry Steel did a joint design venture based on an Eccles Imperial in 1953, named Imperial Knight. The venture was not repeated.

48

The days of luxury showman caravans were over after 1939.

The first name — and the last word in caravans

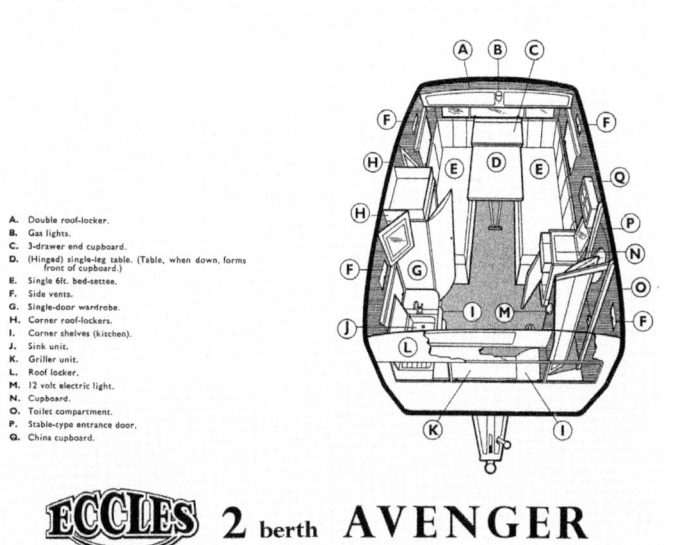

A. Double roof-locker.
B. Gas lights.
C. 3-drawer end cupboard.
D. (Hinged) single-leg table. (Table, when down, forms front of cupboard.)
E. Single 6ft. bed-settee.
F. Side vents.
G. Single-door wardrobe.
H. Corner roof-lockers.
I. Corner shelves (kitchen).
J. Sink unit.
K. Griller unit.
L. Roof locker.
M. 12 volt electric light.
N. Cupboard.
O. Toilet compartment.
P. Stable-type entrance door.
Q. China cupboard.

The Avenger was popular as a family tourer but a two-berth was also available from 1959.

ECCLES 2 berth **AVENGER**

NIPPER

8ft 6in long
2—3 berth

Left: The Eccles Nipper was a micro 2/3-berth lightweight tourer for 1959.

Below: The 1959 Avenger family model was 12 ft in length and cost £315 new.

AVENGER

Chapter Three

Eccles, a New Era

The 1960s was a new decade and one that would project the Eccles name to the fore. Late in 1959, with no new Riley family members coming through, Bill Riley looked at selling the company. In the meantime, Sam Alper, the founder of Sprite Caravans – the 'newbie' of the industry who began in 1948 and had seen a rapid growth of sales with his Sprite range from 1949 – had been an admirer of the Eccles brand and its heritage over the years. He knew Riley and when he heard the company was possibly up for sale, Alper realised this was an opportunity for him to purchase the manufacturer that invented car-pulled caravans and motorhomes, with a well-respected name in the European caravan industry.

One of the last specials from the old Eccles company, built for the Birmingham hospital authority in 1960.

Alper approached Eccles in early 1960 and a deal was done; the Sprite Group was formed and old Eccles customers were horrified that the budget manufacturer Sprite had the Eccles brand. What would happen next? Would Eccles become another Sprite range? Alper knew better and with a strong team the Eccles line-up was looked at closely. Sales had slipped and Eccles had lost their lead; there was no getting away from this. Alper would look at a complete redesign and one that would basically blow the competition away with its exterior and interior features. For 1960, Eccles had eleven models in its line-up, including a new, larger model – the Elegance. Avenger, Nymphette and Landfarer were the other models in the new decade's line-up.

The Eccles Elegance, launched for 1960.

The Landfarer from 1961 was one of the last Birmingham Eccles.

The Eccles Avenger had sold well but 1961 was its final year.

The Birmingham plant was kept on – then disaster struck, or seemed as though it could with Sprite Ltd running in financial meltdown. Alper had overstretched himself, but sales were good; what would he do with creditors snapping at his heals? Alper called for a meeting at Sprite's Newmarket base and told his creditors that sales were high and with the Eccles brand being redeveloped he would be able to pay any debts off with little problem. Sam Alper was a good communicator and after the meeting he was voted to be given more time, which paid off and seemingly put to rest the worries of creditors a year later.

In 1961, the Eccles line-up was reduced to six models that would include a new micro 10 ft tourer, the Echo, designed basically for the German market. The Echo was designed to be towed by the VW Beatle and the BMC Austin Mini car, but it was to last just a season. Also the next big news was that the Eccles manufacturing plant was to be moved to Newmarket. A few miles from Sprite, at a new factory that was designed to be more efficient and with the old factories sold off, the move was made. But the big news wasn't to end there, because the job of redesigning the Eccles range was given to a new man on the scene, Reg Dean. Dean would turn out to be very gifted at contemporary caravan exteriors and interior design.

Dean had been taken on by Alper to bring new ideas into the Sprite Group and his quest was to keep the quality of Eccles, bring it up to date and also make it a profile that stood out from the now ever-growing tourer market. With the new factory (The Pines) on Fordham Road set up, the new 'Newmarket-look Eccles' were ready to roll and make their debut. There were three new models: the GT305, a 10 ft four-berth; 13 ft four-berth Moonstone and the 16 ft Sapphire, plus the ever reliable Eccles Traveller left over from the old range. The new models had sloping rear and front ends and a new curved roof line plus a bay front window and pelmet designs over the exterior side windows. By 1964, the GT305 was to adopt the Sprite 400 body, which was more pleasing to the eye overall than the original launch version.

The interiors were minimal with a light finish for the walls, and while overall storage was more restricted, the new Eccles models certainly looked larger inside than the lengths they actually were. New-look furniture saw wood finish only on the wardrobe or cupboard

53

The Echo was built for the new breed of small cars such as the Beetle.

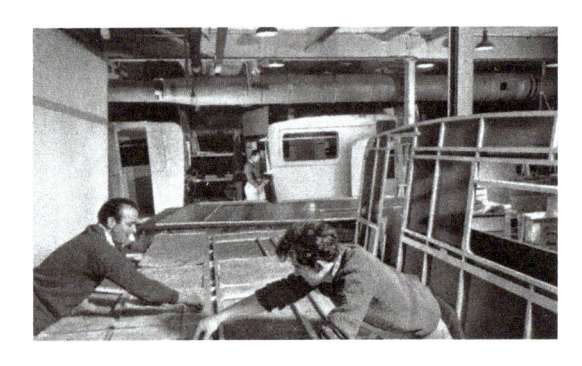

Producing the 'Newmarket Eccles' at the Pines factory in 1962.

The 1962 brochure shows the evolution of the Eccles brand.

An Eccles Moonstone in production at the Pines factory. Seven years later the Fairholme range of tourers would be built in the Pines factory too.

The Eccles GT305 from 1962; it was used in the Tin Tin *Black Island* book and also a model made available until around 2002.

C   Table
E   Floor locker
F   Dinette seats
G   Wardrobe
H   Kitchen unit
I   Crockery cupboard
N   Single bed/bunk over
T   Door mat
☼   Gas lights

1964; the GT305 borrowed its bodyshell from the Sprite 400.

55

doors. By 1963, the 22 ft Emerald was launched as a large tourer for showmen or used as a holiday van to be left on-site. The new factory was able to turn out 1,500 tourers a year yet retain the Eccles quality, which Sam Alper was keen to do. Eccles had to retain its upmarket stance as well as be innovative in design.

But the Eccles brand was to get another owner. The new company would be Caravans International, with the merger of Bluebird Caravans and Motorhomes. Eccles was now in the largest group in the UK and eventually Europe. In October 1963 the company was formed and Eccles was now classed as Sprite, a partner in Caravans International (or by 1967, Ci). At the merger the company had orders for 7,157 caravans valued at £1.8 million, all taken at the Earls Court Show.

Eccles would be seen throughout Europe and, with advanced use of plastics with a special vacuum-forming plant, Eccles could produce all types of plastic parts for the vans. This new technology would see more plastic mouldings being used by the 1967 Eccles range, with front bay windows used as a one-piece moulded unit. Other plastic components were made for other Ci models at the Pines.

The Eccles profile was firmly established and detailed improvements would be carried out but its designer Reg Dean decided that he wanted a new challenge and, much to Sam Alper's surprise, left to join a small maker in Manchester – Lynton Caravans. Dean would

The Pines factory was a few miles from Sprite; Eccles were kept very separate.

Eccles make their own vacuum formed plastic components for caravans.

Eccles had high-tech plastic moulding machines by the mid '60s.

further develop the same sort of modern trends in design that he had done for Eccles, making the Lynton brand stand out from the crowd and a successful touring range.

The Eccles range from 1962 would now be built on the Sprite chassis and with the new Ci group, more money could go into new ideas and development. Stability on tow was proven when an Eccles Moonstone towed by a Jensen CV8 sports car officially hit 97 mph – more proof of Eccles' high-speed towing capabilities. Dean may have left, but with a dedicated design team the Eccles brand was moving on over the coming years.

The 1965 Moonstone had two layouts, one with tip-up double bed the other with rear end bunk beds. The Sapphire too would have two layouts: De-Luxe and De-Luxe tip-up. Prices

The 1965 Eccles Sapphire with its distinctive profile; the cost was £500.

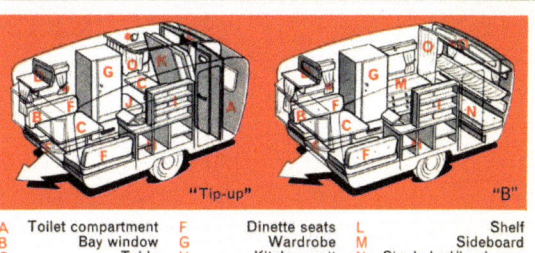

The two Moonstone layouts for 1965, costing £430–£435.

A	Toilet compartment	F	Dinette seats	L	Shelf
B	Bay window	G	Wardrobe	M	Sideboard
C	Table	H	Kitchen unit	N	Single bed/bunk over
D	Roof locker	I	Crockery cupboard	O	Dividing curtain
E	Floor locker	J	Small dinette seat	•	Gas light
		K	Tip-up bed		

57

ranged from £285 to £695 for the Emerald. The Pines factory was producing nearly 2,000 Eccles caravans a year by 1966 and with Sprite's output the pair were awarded the coveted Queens Award for exports. Eccles had witnessed good success in the British Caravan Road Rallies in 1961/63 and '68, winning various trophies.

A tour of Scandinavia and Sweden in 1965 with a Moonstone and 1925 Eccles and Austin tow car would visit various towns and cities, ending with a stop at the Eccles Swedish importer Ljunggrens. The PR obtained for Eccles helped secure more sales with the modern and vintage outfit tour. No other caravan manufacturer could boast of such a heritage as Eccles.

Eccles were revamped for 1967, with a mock wood grain waistband and moulded front gas locker added for 1968. The Sapphire also became available as a winterised version (Winter Sports) with underfloor insulation, double glazing, and gas convector heater, all to make the Sapphire a year-round tourer. The GT305 had, by 1966, been redesigned using the then-new Sprite 400 Mk3 body, though with a more luxurious interior and also re-named GT306. For 1967 and '68 it would follow as the 307 and 308. The GT would by 1969 become the Opal. The '67 models began another evolution with the Eccles profile and interior originated in 1962. 1968 saw the launch of a new 12 ft two-berth Topaz, further strengthening the Eccles line-up.

The totally new 10 ft four-berth Opal tourer was given a brand-new profile (later used on the 1970 Sprite-400-Alpine) with a new curved roofline. A pre-production Opal was given a pre-production test run with a Triumph GT60 sports car, taking a gruelling 2,000-mile trip through Europe that averaged 47 mph over 42 hours. The next test was an endurance run with 23-year-old rally driver Liz Firmin. Using an Alfa Romeo 1750 saloon, Liz drove from

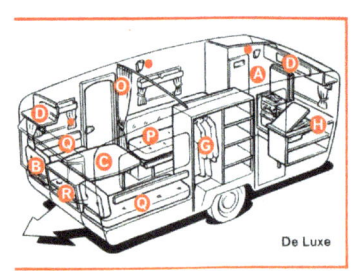

De Luxe

Dimensions, Shipping sizes, Under gear, Body construction, Windows and Ventilation, Exterior lighting, Interior and Exterior finish as De Luxe model.
Weight: 16¼ cwt.

Equipment
Foam bedding with spring interior tip-up bed mattress. 50 mm. towing ball. Leg brace. Full oven cooker. Three gas lights. Division curtain. Gas bottle mounting. Screw type jockey wheel. Carpet. Wheel embellishers. Berth lamp. Mirror.

Interior Lay-out
Two single beds with cocktail cabinet and table between. Tip-up bed. End kitchen. Wardrobe. Mirror. Day seat. Rear toilet compartment. Full width front locker. Rear locker and shelf over kitchen unit.

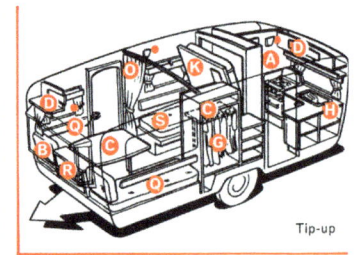

Tip-up

A—Toilet compartment B—Bay window C—Table
D—Roof locker G—Wardrobe H—Kitchen unit
O—Dividing curtain P—Double bed settee Q—Single beds R—Cocktail cabinet •—Gas lights

A—Toilet compartment B—Bay window C—Tab
D—Roof locker G—Wardrobe H—Kitchen un
K—Tip-up bed O—Dividing curtain Q—Single bec
R—Cocktail cabinet S—Day seat •—Gas lights

Sapphire Tip-up interior ▶
◀ Sapphire de-luxe interior

1966 Sapphire layouts; note the contemporary interior – a Dean speciality.

58

Here, roof beams are glued, formed under pressure and laminated by high frequency radio beams, giving outstanding strength and lightness.

Aluminium sheet is cut to pattern – six sheets at a time. Aluminium is used, of course, for its light weight and corrosion-resistant qualities.

Glass fibre insulation protects the walls of every tourer against extreme temperatures.

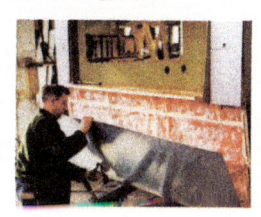

This is the machine which we have recently installed to mould thermoplastic cutlery and crockery holders, wheel arch assemblies and bay window surrounds.

Roofs, too, receive a layer of glass fibre insulation. The process of laying the 'blanket' calls for craftsman's skill and care.

A modern paradox; all furniture in the 1968 tourers is now wax polished by hand.

Aluminium comes into its own time and time again in the Eccles manufacturing process. Here racks of aluminium gutter mouldings 'frame' a Sapphire about to take its turn in the paint shop.

Hot spray paint process with infra-red accelerated drying ensures a consistently fine finish.

The manufacturing process from 1968 at the Pines plant.

The 1962/3 Eccles Moonstone with Triumph Herald convertible at the British Caravan Road Rally.

59

Here's what makes ECCLES 1st Class...

1. Thermoplastic gas bottle cover
2. Thermoplastic bay window surround
3. Transparent draught-proof window ventilators
4. Corrosion-resistant wheel arches in thermoplastic
5. Plastic curtain rails
6. Cut-pile, fitted carpet
7. Coconut doormat
8. Hydraulically damped hitch
9. Weatherproof hook-lapped roof joints
10. Combined gutter/awning rail
11. Simulated wood waist band
12. Laminated plastic working surfaces
13. Two-tone Dunlopreme upholstery
14. Moulded plastic cutlery/crockery trays
15. Wipe-clean wall covering
16. Large grab handles
17. Independent suspension
18. Afrormosia veneer furniture
19. Non-perishable rubber draught excluder

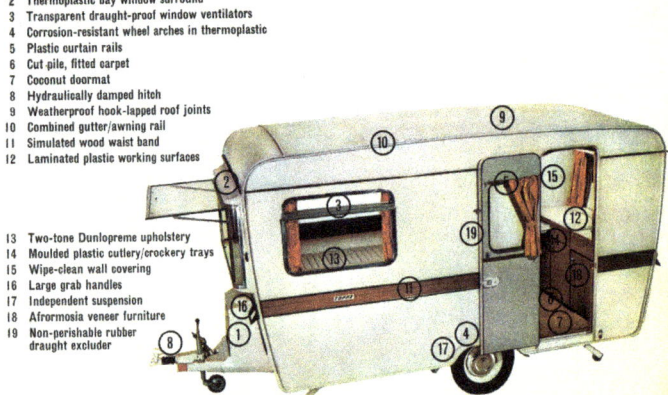

Above: The October 1965 PR trip to Scandinavia with a new and old Eccles. They attracted lots of attention.

Left: Anatomy of the 1968 Eccles tourer (Topaz) showing Eccles features.

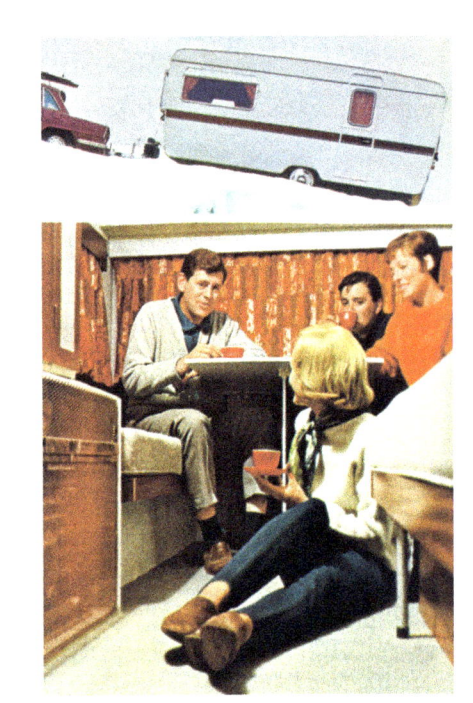

The 1967 Eccles Winter Sports was designed for all-season touring.

ECCLES

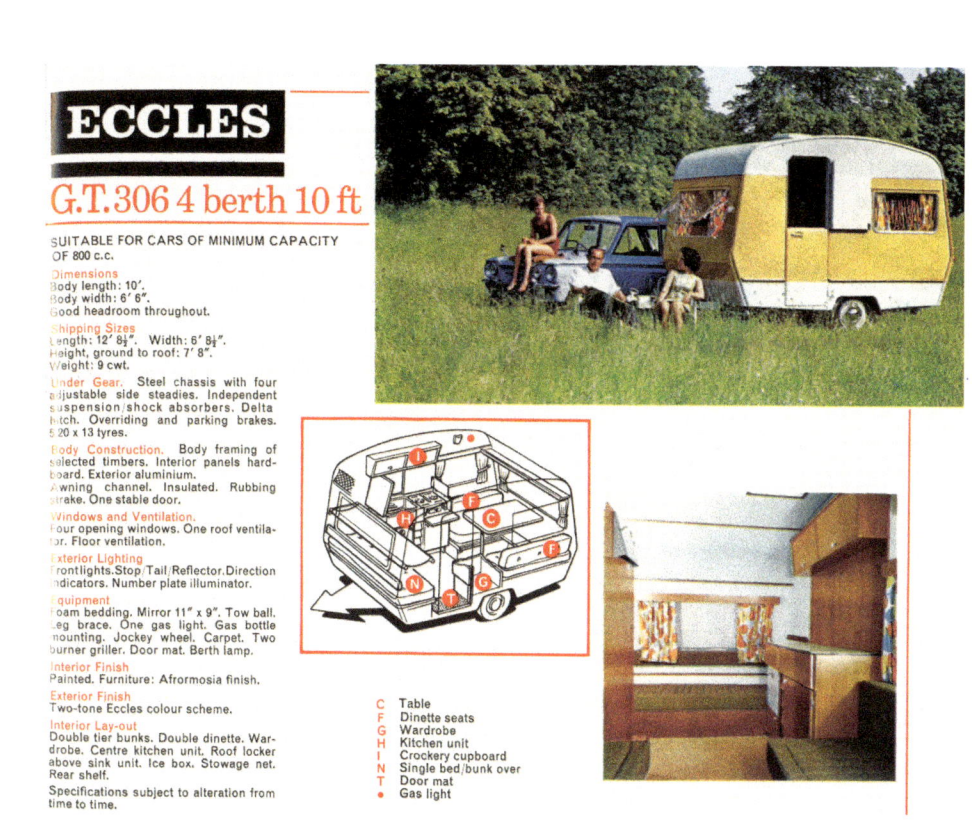

G.T. 306 4 berth 10 ft

SUITABLE FOR CARS OF MINIMUM CAPACITY OF 800 c.c.

Dimensions
Body length: 10'.
Body width: 6' 6".
Good headroom throughout.

Shipping Sizes
Length: 12' 8½". Width: 6' 8½".
Height, ground to roof: 7' 8".
Weight: 9 cwt.

Under Gear. Steel chassis with four adjustable side steadies. Independent suspension/shock absorbers. Delta hitch. Overriding and parking brakes. 5.20 x 13 tyres.

Body Construction. Body framing of selected timbers. Interior panels hardboard. Exterior aluminium. Awning channel. Insulated. Rubbing strake. One stable door.

Windows and Ventilation.
Four opening windows. One roof ventilator. Floor ventilation.

Exterior Lighting
Frontlights. Stop/Tail/Reflector. Direction Indicators. Number plate illuminator.

Equipment
Foam bedding. Mirror 11" x 9". Tow ball. Leg brace. One gas light. Gas bottle mounting. Jockey wheel. Carpet. Two burner griller. Door mat. Berth lamp.

Interior Finish
Painted. Furniture: Afrormosia finish.

Exterior Finish
Two-tone Eccles colour scheme.

Interior Lay-out
Double tier bunks. Double dinette. Wardrobe. Centre kitchen unit. Roof locker above sink unit. Ice box. Stowage net. Rear shelf.

Specifications subject to alteration from time to time.

- C Table
- F Dinette seats
- G Wardrobe
- H Kitchen unit
- I Crockery cupboard
- N Single bed/bunk over
- T Door mat
- • Gas light

The 1966 Eccles, renamed GT 306, borrowed the bodyshell from the then-new Mk 3 Sprite 400.

Interior of the new 1968 Topaz two-berth; interiors had been restyled in 1967.

The Triumph GT6 towed the Opal 2,000 miles in 42 hours—average 47·6

Above left: The 1969 Opal replaced GT308; the new profile would be used for the Sprite 400/Alpin from 1970.

Above right: Prototype 1969 Opal, tested on an endurance run over 2,000 miles in Europe.

Liz Firmin, twenty-three, begins her non-stop London to Rome trip in 1968.

London to Rome (1,188 miles) in just short of 24 hours! Average speed was 50 plus mph and the Opal came through with flying colours!

In 1967, with three 1968 Eccles tourers and in conjunction with Mobil Oil, a test of towing petrol consumption was carried out on both a track and a 213-mile round trip on motorways and B roads. The Eccles tourers proved economical to tow and furthermore the Eccles tourers were lightweight yet well-equipped for that period. The following year, 1969, would be a very important one for the Eccles brand. But before this big year, in 1968 Bill Riley sadly passed away; the industry had lost a pioneer and the man who, with his father, had invented commercial caravanning. The following year was the 50th anniversary of Eccles and a large rally was organised for Eccles owners at Newmarket, where the Owners Club was reformed.

Also, the rally saw a good gathering of Eccles tourers from as far back as the early 1920s. A cavalcade through Newmarket (beginning at Edgbaston, Birmingham) brought out the

Above left: Eccles led the way with Mobile Oil on an economy towing trip.

Above right: The booklet printed for the occasion was priced at 2s 6d (12.5p).

The weekend noted a good turnout of classic Eccles, including the restored 1928 Eccles and 1937 Triumph Gloria owned by Glyn Lancaster Jones.

ECCLES MILESTONE

A small sector of the rally. In the front row, left to right, are the 1948 Enterprise, M. Rochat's 1928 van towed from Switzerland, and the concours-winning 1928 Jacobean

The rally field in 1969 for Eccles owners; the owners club was reformed.

Special cavalcade for Eccles' 50 years Golden Jubilee.

crowds and plenty of outfits for the Golden Jubilee Rally at Newmarket. 1969 was also the year that the Ogle Design group with Tom Karen designed a brand-new model for 1970. The Amethyst used extensive plastic mouldings for the roof and front and rear panels. The chassis finished at the axle and the interior boasted Eccles design flair with a contemporary finish. The model had been extensively tested over 10,000 miles and was launched at the Earls Court Caravan Show in November 1969 to a great reception from Eccles dealers. With business booming, Eccles required more staff. The company advertised in the local paper, announcing vacancies at the Pines Eccles factory.

With the new Ogle-designed Amethyst, Eccles was the talk of the caravan industry and the public. By 1971 there had been some changes to the 1970 Amethyst; a full chassis was back while the side gas locker remained. All but the Sapphire received the new Ogle look but by 1972 that was rectified. The Emerald 22 ft holiday tourer had been dropped for 1971 and the Opal received a new front-hood-type moulded plastic front panel. By 1972 all the

The new Amethyst model was brimming with innovative ideas.

A. Toilet/Shower compartment
B. Front window
C. Table
D. Roof locker
E. Floor lockers
F. Wardrobe
G. Kitchen unit
I. Dividing curtain
L. Double bed/settee/single bunk over
O. Dinette seats with backrests making double bed
Q. Crockery cupboard
R. Cupboards
S. Pelma-vent shelves
T. Gas bottle compartment (built into wardrobe base, access from outside)
X. Gas light
Y. Electric lights (12v.)

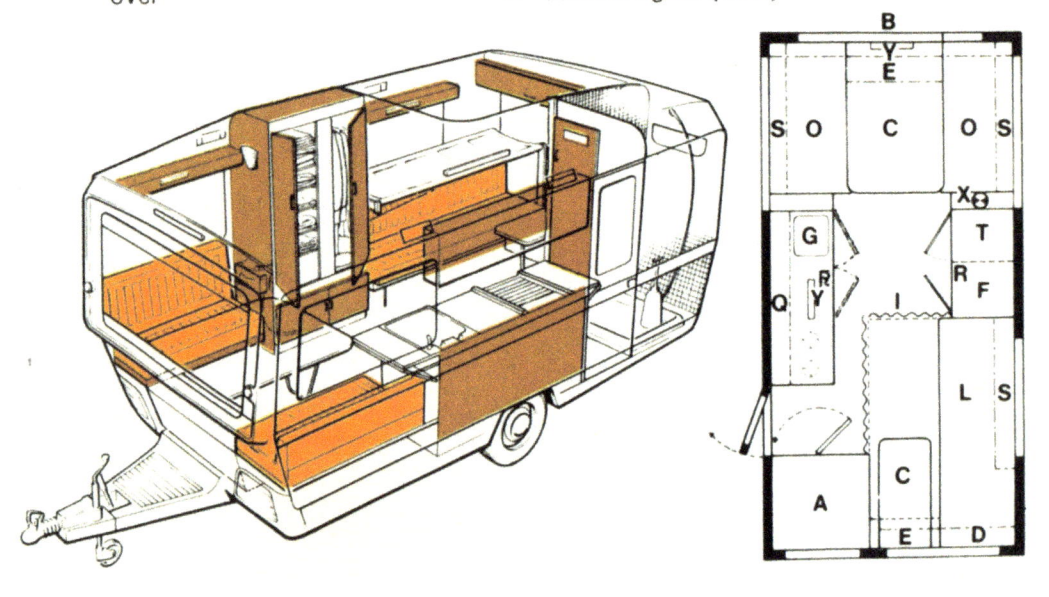

Over 14 ft long, the Amethyst came complete with a shower where the water was hand-pumped!

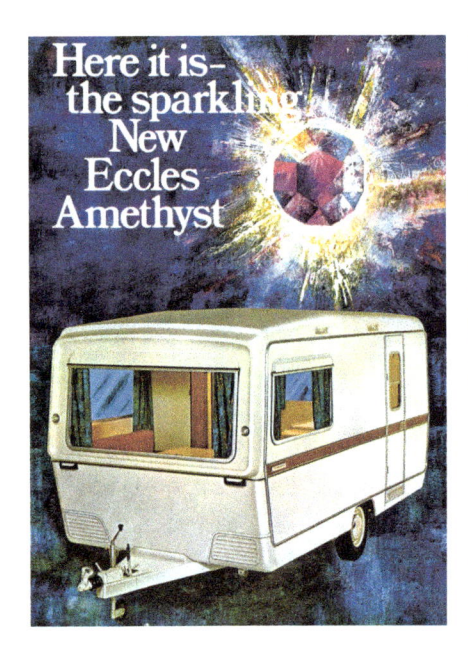

Above: Part of the pre-production Amethyst 10,000-mile testing in early '69.

Left: November 1969 saw the Ogle Design group develop the new Eccles, which was seen as a breakthrough in many areas.

66

Above: The big 22 ft Emerald from 1969 was dropped by 1971.

Right: The late '60s and early '70s was boom time; Eccles were always recruiting!

Ask any man . . .

who works at Eccles and he'll tell you it's a fine Company. They build some of the best luxury touring caravans in the world—not surprising they hold the Queen's Award. And now they need more men, men like you, to help them.

IMMEDIATE VACANCIES

Wood Machinists
Trainee Caravan Assemblers
Nightwatchman
Young Man (17-20)

for clerical duties in Maintenance Control Dept.

Good rates of pay. 3 weeks annual paid holiday Excellent conditions of employment.
Make a move NOW and look forward to a brighter 1970.
Write, call or phone our Personnel Office at Fordham 481

**ECCLES CARAVANS, THE PINES
FORDHAM ROAD, NEWMARKET**

ECCLES

cn6

The 1972 Eccles Topaz was all the range; it had the Ogle treatment.

67

Eccles range now had the Ogle look and the Opal was also dropped. It was in 1972 that the decision was made that the Ci Group should operate a proprietary dealer network selling Sprite, Europa, Eccles and Fairholme.

With dealers dedicated to Ci tourers, parts and promotions would be backed by the company. Eccles would benefit from this move and PR events saw Eccles further marketed, with exports still riding high. One Ci marketing move was to place the latest 1972 models at one of London's railway stations. With a brochure desk and information, the Eccles created some new sales off the venture. The company also used an Eccles cut in half, which viewers walked through the middle so they could see the interior better; again it was placed on a station platform and created a lot of enquirers for the Eccles brand.

From the end of '72 Ci went solo, selling just the Ci brands including Eccles; they could sell a non-competitive luxury brand too.

The 1972 Eccles on display at a London train station; bringing caravans to non-caravanners proved a profitable idea.

The mid-70s would see sales of all makes hit by the oil crisis and inflation. VAT was also added in 1973 and to keep prices competative the Ci Group would try to cut its production costs. The 1973 Eccles range received new exterior colours but sales were slowing generally for Eccles tourers; however, TV star Victor Madden purchased a Sapphire from his local Ci dealer that year. The Eccles was now looking quite dated both inside and out; the profile looked very boxy and the build quality wasn't up to Eccles standards. The interiors had gone more mainstream by 1975 but the Ci design team were to work hard on a new Eccles. In the meantime a 1926 Eccles had been found and taken to the Ci Eccles plant. It was from here that talks began with Beaulieu motor museum in 1974–75 regarding donating the Eccles fully restored.

TV star of the '70s Victor Madden with his wife and their new 1973 Sapphire.

1973 Sapphire interior with strong 1970s fashion colour treatment!

There was more work needed than first thought; the Ci team realised it needed new panels, framing, interior and stove adding. Caravan Service at Isleham in Cambridgeshire would carry out the work. Experts Glyn Lancaster Jones and Harold Catt (founders of the Historic Caravan Register) were brought in to consult on authentic items and age. The original cost of £480 went up to £612.70, the work was finished and the Eccles was delivered and has stayed ever since at the museum, still on full display in 2017. In 1975 the film *Carry On Behind* was made, with Ci supplying caravans for the film set. Eccles of course featured strongly, again giving the brand more publicity. The film was a big success and featured all the Carry On stars.

The new Eccles launch was in 1976 – a more conventional profile using a typical clubman profile plus a new more modern interior. A new foam-injected sandwich construction was now also used by Ci after using it on the Ci Europa range a few years earlier with success.

The written quote for the 1926 restored Eccles for Beaulieu motor museum from 1975. The Eccles was from Sam Alper's private collection.

Above: Actor Kenneth Connor with an Eccles Topaz on the set of *Carry on Behind* in 1975.

Right: The 1926 Eccles still on public display in 2017 at Beaulieu National Motor Museum.

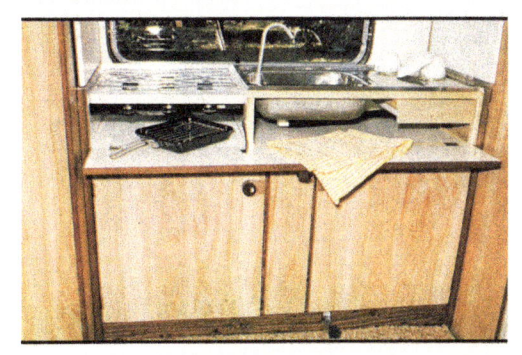

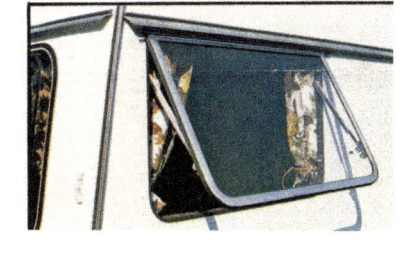

The new 1976 Eccles reverted to a more traditional profile but had new construction and interiors.

71

SUPERCARE SERVICE

Every Eccles caravan is backed by Supercare, the most complete caravan after-sales service in the world. And that service begins the moment you tow your caravan away.

FULL 12 MONTH WARRANTY
Not just a piece of paper but a complete guarantee covering both parts and labour and which even includes items such as curtains, carpets and cushions. Your CI Dealer will be happy to tell you exactly what it covers.

SECOND-YEAR WARRANTY INSURANCE*
Included in your purchase price, and upon registration, a Lloyd's insurance covering the major parts for a further year, right up to £500 in total. PLUS the opportunity to continue the insurance at a privileged price.

PARTS & SERVICE GUARANTEED
At Supercare Centres you'll find service men who have been trained in Eccles construction and maintenance. And every replacement part you are likely to need has been catalogued for speed and safety... every part approved by CI.

TOW PLAN*
For a nominal sum you can enjoy the benefit of the CI Caravans Towing Protection Plan. Details available from your nearest CI Dealer. The complete Supercare Service is operated through over 130 Centres throughout Britain.

No other caravan manufacturer offers such a comprehensive service.

*Not available in Eire.

CI CARAVANS

Above: Looking towards rear end of Elan 14

Above: Fridge unit in Elan 14

Above: The new super luxury Eccles Élans were launched for 1978 and were well-specified.

Left: Eccles, as part of Ci, benefited from the innovative back-up warranties introduced in the late '70s.

The new-look Eccles took off but the range had been cut back; the Sapphire was dropped after thirteen years. The new Eccles regained their position and the four-model range sold well even in a tough market. Eccles would also benefit from the new Ci extended warranty scheme, introduced in March 1977. Named Vanguard, it offered a second year of cover for little extra cost, a first in the caravan industry. Vanguard was later to be re-branded as Supercare.

The Ci proprietary dealerships could also offer this on used models too. By 1978 new updated interiors were added but the Topaz and Amethyst in several layouts, including the two-berth Topaz, still stood firm. The big news for that year was the new luxury Eccles Élan two-model range; the 12 and 14, based on the Topaz-2 and Amethyst, featured Swedish-made Bofors double glazing, oven, fridge, and flued heater with thermostat control. Prices were £2,377 and £2,586 but the new luxury Élans would prove a hit with experienced caravanners.

1979 was to see a recession and sales in the industry would suffer, with caravan manufacturers struggling and going out of business in many cases. Even Ci would feel the pinch as exports began to dry up and its factories in Europe were over-producing other Ci ranges. Eccles, in the meantime, was still a leader and with Ci as a parent company the benefits were considerable. The 1979 Eccles range was upgraded and now included a fridge as standard while another Élan 14 was added to the range. The next decades would bring mixed fortunes but would see Eccles still as a leader in design.

Chapter Four

Eccles Leads into the '80s and Beyond

With the UK economy looking grim, the sales of new touring caravans were slow, and with more competition the Ci group was struggling. The main competitor was the Beverley-based ABI Caravans, a company that had, like Ci, developed various brands off its initial Ace range of mid-market tourers. ABI had become second to Ci after growing and being price conscious, meeting every price point on the touring market. The ABI brands that were gunning for Eccles and the Eccles Élans were the Ace and Ace Awards. Prices between the two were very close and in 1980 the Award was £3,577 – the same as the Élan 14! The Award and Aces lagged behind with construction and it would take them another three years to catch up to Ci with sandwich-bonded sides. But they were catching up with more ABI dealerships being added.

However, along with the other brands Eccles was still being enhanced for the new decade and the brand was on the short list for many caravanners wanting lightweight, quality, well-specified tourers. A choice of soft furnishings was available and four Eccles models still were in the line up; the Élans had just two layouts – the 12 and 14. Few changes were made for 1981 as the Ci Company were trying to sell off some of the foreign concerns and

Eccles had a new main competitor from ABI – the Ace range in 1980.

The Acc Award range competed head-on with the Eccles Élans; ABI was the UK's second biggest manufacturer of caravans after Ci.

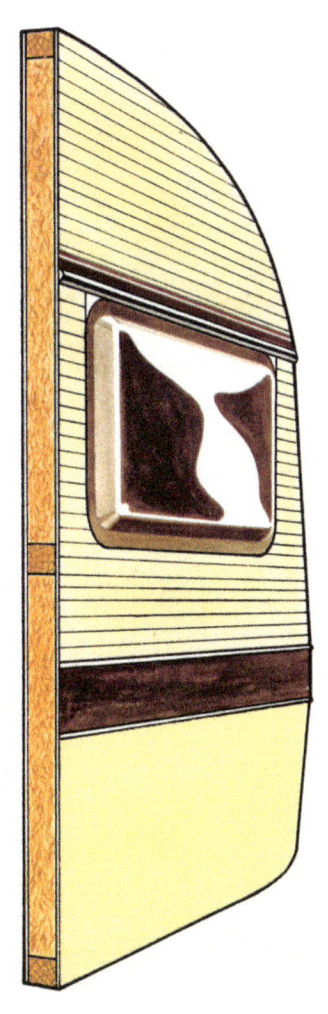

Above left: The Eccles Topaz was one of Eccles' best-selling models in 1980.

Above right: Eccles bonded construction used Styrofoam injected into the sides and floor.

UK ones too. OBI awnings, part of the Ci group, for some years had tailor-made awnings to fit all the Ci range, including Eccles, and Ci also had 130 dedicated dealers stocking all the parts most Ci customers would require. Ci was still the leader and Eccles was one of the main brands but losses and borrowing were jeopardising the business.

Above left: The 1980 Eccles Élan 2 boasted a good specification and cost £3,234.

Above right: Topaz offered families a medium-priced lightweight tourer.

Left: Ci Caravans had a brochure with all the spares/options available from their proprietary dealerships, which included parts for Eccles models too.

1982 would be the Caravan Club's (now named Caravan and Motorhome Club) 75th anniversary. It seemed a good occasion for Ci to help with a special tourer and what better than an Eccles Élan 14 complete with stereo radio and cassette fitted? Both the Club and Eccles could boast over sixty years in existence. To top the offer and the Club winner of the Élan, Mantles Caravans dealership also included an OBI awning worth over £300. Celebrations were to be relatively short-lived at Ci though, as the bank threatened to pull the plug. However, the 1983 season saw new models with a new Amethyst being added – another family model.

In December 1982, after the Earls Court Show, Ci went into liquidation, taking Eccles with it. Alper was almost shunned and by February 1983 a management buyout was complete, with Sam Alper not involved. Leaner and with a far smaller workforce and factory, the Eccles brand was back in production. The oldest name in the world of caravans was still in business. With sales picking up generally, the new Ci team wasted little time developing the ranges. By 1984 the Élans had lost their Eccles badge but they were still Eccles. With mains electrics added and new interiors for both the Eccles standard and Élan, sales proved good. The Ci proprietary dealership dissolved but many old Ci dealers stayed on. The Super care and Ci Finance had dissolved with the old Ci.

Above left: A 1982 Eccles Élan 14 was offered in a competition for the then Caravan Club's 75th anniversary. (Photo courtesy of Garry Batten)

Above right: The 1983 Eccles line-up was launched in September 1982, but by December Ci had gone – would Eccles survive?

77

New wheel spats and trim.

Raked seats with smooth, snag-free end panels.

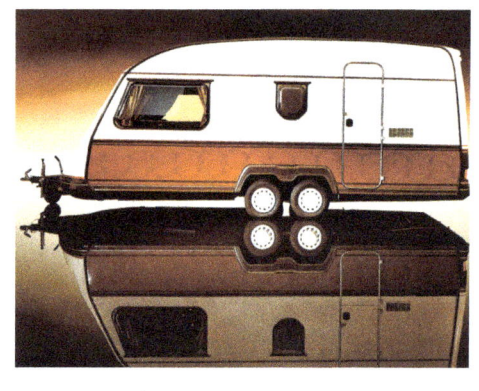

Moulded washroom sections 1, 2 and 3 are in the Eccles (2 only in Topaz S). Élans have sections 1–4.

Above: The Élan for 1985 was stunning and developed under a new Ci.

Left: The 1983 Eccles had undergone big improvements, including the Ci moulded washroom optional add-ons.

The Élan was highly specified but sales were not as hoped.

Profits reinvested saw some striking designs and none more so than the 1985 Élans. A stunning aerodynamic profile with luxury interiors and a high spec made these tourers real head-turners, featuring an integral front gas locker and even a rear storage boot integral in the full-height moulded panel, plus full mains electrics and two twin-axled models, all on fully galvanised chassis. The new Élans, were available in four layouts, but sales proved poor. The 85 Eccles range basically stuck to its profile, now in its ninth year though with alterations in that time. The caravan press saw the new Eccles as a good range with any tests being given a positive slant.

Above: The 1985 Eccles relied heavily on the 1976 profile.

Right: 1987 the Eccles ranges had a full revamp, which proved a hit with buyers.

1986 saw the Eccles Élan's traditional profile with triple windows and large gas locker, but again sales were sluggish.

The Élan would be dropped and replaced by the new Elite – basically an Élan but based on the Eccles' new 1986 look, which came with massive front and dated gas locker. Triple front windows echoed clubman appeal and the new separate Ci Elite range was obviously higher specified but shared the Eccles profile. But the 1986 Eccles models looked dated and sales reflected this. By 1987 a new aerodynamic Eccles emerged from Newmarket; with new moulded front and rear panels, the profile was influenced by strong wind tunnel testing during 1986.

The 1987 layout choices were popular with caravanners and were chosen exactly for that reason. Interestingly, the export market for the Eccles brand was also proving a success, especially with the newly designed Eccles profile with all its added specification. Two old names – Sapphire and Moonstone – also made a comeback for 1987. The Elites would be known as Eccles Elite, offering more luxury fittings and higher spec than the base models.

Above: Sprite Leisure's Eccles range from 1992. The last Ci in 1989 had won the Queens Award for Exports with its Sprite range.

Left: Eccles exports were always good – 1988 Eccles built for the Dutch market.

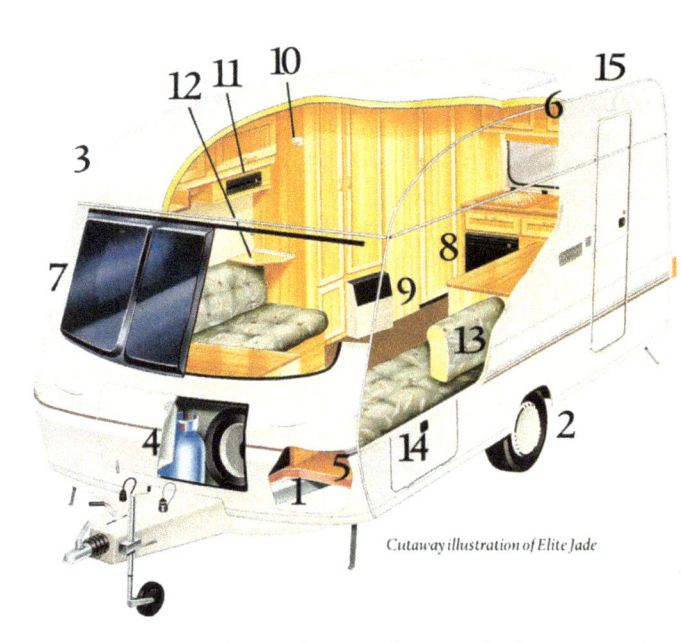

1 Exceptionally strong, fully galvanised chassis, uniquely designed and manufactured at our factory.
2 Top quality radial tyres; independent Knott Rubber Torsion Bar suspension and auto-reverse mechanism.
3 Aerodynamic styling for extra stability and reduction of wind resistance.
4 Fully integrated gas bottle storage area with additional space for a spare wheel; 12V courtesy light included.
5 40mm thick bonded styrene floor.
6 Fully insulated roof cavity; 26mm bonded styrene side and end walls.
7 Double glazed tinted acrylic windows.
8 Fully equipped kitchen area with Electrolux refrigerator; moulded sink and drainer unit; matching vitreous enamel grill and 3-burner hotplate with glass lid; Monte Carlo oven.
9 Carver Carvelle M space heater.
10 Control switch for Carver Cascade hot water system and shower.
11 Zig CF 2000 charging and distribution system.
12 Drop down TV table.
13 Luxurious velour upholstery.
14 Outside access storage locker.
15 Awning light.

Cutaway illustration of Elite Jade

Eccles Elite exploded view showing the extra high spec in 1987.

The end of the '80s had proved successful for the Ci Eccles but a small downturn in 1991 would see the Eccles name threatened again but a management buyout saved the day. In fact the Elites, which were better specified, were selling better than the standard Eccles range and for 1990 four Eccles models were available. By 1991 it was decided that the Eccles name should be put to one side and the brand Elite used instead; also the jewel names were dropped for model designation and numbers were used. The Elite SE was introduced to replace the previous year's Elite. But the Eccles name was quickly re-introduced for 1992; Ci also stopped chassis production and brought in BPW while a new management team re-named the company Sprite Leisure.

New development and big investment in new CAD systems and machinery and the standard fitting of the Tyron safety bands for blowouts was all part of the new Sprite Leisure forward thinking. Eccles was back and selling well. After 1992, the SE badge was attached and the specification upgraded and by 1994 Eccles were renamed Elite.

The big news then was that the Sprite Leisure Group was in line for another change of ownership. The Eccles name was sold to the Yorkshire-based Swift Group by mid-1994 in

Above: New investment by Sprite Leisure in CAD design helped developing the Eccles models.

Right: Some of the features of the 1995 Eccles including rear bike carrier.

81

the next part of the Eccles story. Just before this happened, a customer with a 1988 Eccles had toured the UK and Europe over several years. When the Newmarket factory checked the Eccles over they found all that was needed was a new jockey wheel – proof that Eccles was still a quality range of durable tourers.

Swift would then buy the Newmarket factory and all stock and take over manufacturing of the other brands, Sprite and Europa, too. Sprite Leisure as a brand was dropped and a new name was used – Sterling Caravans. The Newmarket factory was sadly closed in the summer of 1995, though the 1996 prototypes were built there. After thirty-four years the Eccles brand was moved to Swift's new factory extension at Cottingham. Swift would now look at developing the Eccles touring range; it was almost a repeat of history, with Eccles becoming part of a large caravan manufacturing concern. Owner of Swift Group Peter Smith was keen to keep the Eccles name very much alive, knowing full well, as Sam Alper had done in 1960, the innovative flair of Eccles and of course respect for the oldest name in the business.

Into 1996, Eccles was to now have seven layouts and the future looked secure again for the brand. An altered profile added a fresh look as well as a new interior, along with a new

ECCLES ELITE

1995 and one of the last Eccles caravans built at Newmarket after Swift purchased the company in 1994.

1996 Eccles interior – the new Sterling Eccles had been built at Cottingham's Swift Groups plant.

twin-axled Explorer layout being added. The latest Eccles got the thumbs up and the owners club (www.ecclescoc.co.uk) accepted the new Sterling Eccles tourers into the club. Exports would, as previously, still become part of the Eccles market under the Swift Group. Swift would further develop Eccles tourers with newly designed washrooms in 1997, and by 1998 a total of four twin-axled Eccles were available. By 1999 the Eccles range totalled fourteen layouts!

The new decade would see some big improvements and Eccles would receive a new identity of flair and design – Eccles forward-thinking of the '60s and '70s was going to return. The brand would set new standards, giving the Eccles ranges a stronger presence in the tourer market. 2000 saw the first fixed bed Eccles layout with the Onyx and the Eccles

The Eccles twin-axled Explorer 580 from 1998 cost £13,895.

Above left: The new 1999 Eccles Elite Trekker interior – a family model.

Above right: The 2001 Eccles Moonstone interior with the new Tecnoform designer Italian furniture – Eccles was finding its identity again.

Elite twin-axled Searcher, introducing continental-styled layouts, was also used with new Italian designer Tecnoform furniture and Belgian fabrics. Flair in design was back with the Eccles ranges and sales proved the new look worked well.

By 2002 Sterling Eccles had another interior revamp, leaning more towards a continental interior design with new locker design with silver edging and light apple finish furniture. Specifications were upgraded across the two Eccles ranges. There had been a downturn in sales in 2000–2, but by 2003 onwards sales of touring caravans were increasing. The major shows at Earls Court and the NEC were proving ever more popular, with sales reflecting the public's mood towards the caravanning lifestyle. The Eccles brand under Swift had witnessed strong sales success. In the meantime Swift had the chance to purchase a classic 1938 Eccles Senator, which they would eventually restore to its former glory.

Above left: Eccles Elite Searcher fixed bed in 2001 cost £16,245.

Above right: The 2002 Eccles Amber showing 'Continental influence' with L shaped lounge area.

The 2002 Eccles Emerald exterior; the four berth with end washroom was a popular model in the Eccles range.

Above left: The 1938 Eccles Senator being restored at the Swift plant.

Above right: The Senator's interior was also fully restored to new condition.

Restored, the Eccles was used for shows and dealer events as a PR idea, showing viewers the heritage behind the Eccles name.

The Senator was to be displayed at shows and selected Sterling dealerships as a PR feature proving Eccles' heritage as a leading, well-established caravan brand. The renovation would take some years to happen but once it did a quiet area of the Cottingham plant became the restoration workshop. The Senator was restored inside and out and proved a star attraction wherever it has been shown. By 2004, the Eccles and Eccles Elites were given a new front GRP and rear moulding as well as sleeker interiors overall and had their specifications upgraded; the company also had new modern factory operations, keeping quality high in manufacture. All the GRP mouldings were manufactured in the Cottingham plant and by 2006 a new factory extension was built as demand for Swift and Sterling tourers increased.

New plastic frame technology was being used for wall lockers, and seat base lockers too. New dual fuel hobs had been installed since 2003 and new detachable drainer boards had become another feature on Sterling Eccles tourers along with new high-gloss, tough one-piece aluminium sides. The Eccles range had over the last few years found its identity and living up to its heritage background of groundbreaking tourer interiors that appealed to younger caravan buyers. For 2008 the Eccles received a new body shell, with a 2.3 m width to add extra interior space.

Above left: 2004 Eccles had a new exterior with new GRP front and rear mouldings plus new layouts and updated features.

Above right: The new look Eccles from 2008 now had a wider shell with new profile too.

Kitchens in 2008 came well-equipped with a neatly fitted microwave, full ovens and larger fridges.

Above: Elites would now be detached from the Eccles name; for 08 they had silver sides and Alde heating as standard.

Right: 2008 witnessed new walk-in shower cubicles for end washroom models.

In 2009 the Eccles name was ninety years old and this date was added into the exterior graphics.

The new interiors would enhance the feeling of space and modern living, with curved overhead locker design and modern well-equipped kitchens, enforcing the trendsetting appeal of the Eccles brand. The 2008 season also saw the newly designed walk-in showers in washroom models. The Eccles Elites became detached from the Eccles brand (not for the first time!) and for 2008 received Alde wet heating and silver sides, plus new bodyshells and upgraded specifications.

Eccles would celebrate ninety years in 2009; each new Eccles had the '90' badge attached on the side graphics and confusingly, although the Eccles name had come off the Elite range, they too had the '90th' side graphics and also used the Eccles jewel names in kind with the Eccles range. It was as though the Sterling Elites wanted to be a separate luxury brand yet still retain that unofficial Eccles connection. But the Eccles 09 range also received a brand-new interior that verged on the continental taste. It caused a stir for buyers and traders alike with the new blend of contemporary interior design using Oregon pine finish furniture. Fabrics were modern too and the Eccles had a Scandinavian feel to it. New layouts included a fixed bed, single-axle, rear full-width end washroom model – the Eccles Ruby.

87

Above left: Interiors saw a radical new look; not since the 1962 Eccles had such a change been made to the range. Eccles was setting new standards again.

Above right: The Elite interior from 2009 was even more sumptuous and leaned heavily towards the Eccles 90th range.

2011 was another ground-breaking period with the new super sleek-looking Sterling Eccles. The sunroof was optional, as fitted to the right-hand side Eccles.

    The trade thought sales would be very slow, but it seemed the UK caravanning public was waiting for a new, bolder interior and, no surprise, it came from the Sterling Eccles. What the Rileys would have thought of the next new phase in design from Sterling Eccles we will never know, but the new 2011 models would employ a brand-new and groundbreaking profile involving extensive GRP full-height front and rear-moulded aerodynamic panels. The Elite range, now no longer carrying an Eccles badge, was a super luxury line-up that, using the latest computer 3D designs, produced a sensational design.

Above: The new Eccles looked good at the rear as well as the front.

Right: The 2011 models were stunning and set new standards in tourer design – few were ordered with no sunroof though.

By 2012 the sunroof was a standard fit in all Eccles tourers.

The standard Eccles range also carried the same profile, but the Eccles lacked the new-design front sunroof that was in the Elites. However, the option of a sunroof could be added in the Eccles, which most buyers added in the purchase. The new Eccles range interiors also wooed buyers and the new models went down well, though there were problems supplying the new Eccles and also some dealerships were still scant on demonstrators by the end of 2010 and the 2011 model year. Eight layouts with all the famous model names, such as Moonstone, Topaz and Amethyst, showed the strong link to the Eccles heritage.

It was history repeating itself; when, back in 1962, the contemporary 'Newmarket Reg Dean Eccles' were launched, Eccles interiors were ahead with their ultra-modern decor. Eccles were leaders yet again and would also introduce more stunning interiors. New construction would be implemented over the next few years and also the Eccles range would receive a new mid-market range for 2012 – the Eccles Sport. This range would be used by some Sterling dealers to customise for dealer specials.

Interiors of the new Eccles were also impressive.

For 2013 the Eccles was given a new range; named the Sport, it was lightweight and offered decent specifications.

The Eccles SE range replaced the 2012 standard Eccles, sharing the Sports bodyshell.

The Eccles Topaz from 2014 now had the latest SMART construction – the new black front added to its styling too.

The Eccles Sports were placed at mid-market and boasted the new modern interiors of Oregon pine wood finish and would come with a good specification, including ATC from Al-Ko. The jewel names had been replaced by numbers for model designations. The Eccles Sports were carried through to 2013 but the sunroof option was so popular it was now fitted as standard, as too was a tracker system. An upgraded bodyshell-based Eccles Sport named SE was added for 2013, offering the Eccles buyer a new lighter yet well-equipped range that would be towable by most family cars. The SE range also saw the jewel names carry over while Sterling's parent company, Swift, was busy developing new construction methods.

For 2014 the new system was introduced, eliminating timber in the main body. The new system, known as SMART, was arrived at by the following:

Strong – Pure, a hard, polyurethane-based material that won't be damaged with water.
Modern – this new construction allowed Eccles to remain up to date with the most stylish profiles.
Aerodynamic – profiles generated by computer testing for better stability.
Resilient – Pure, a material that is super durable and water resistant.
Tested – track testing at Millbrook and cold chamber testing to -15 degrees.

AERODYNAMIC
We continue to lead the way in Aerodynamics using Computational Fluid Dynamics to help shape the bodyshell for better fuel consumption and safer towing.

RESILIENT
All fixings are made into the 'PURe' material to a pre-defined depth. 'PURe' is totally impervious to water and has no veins. This means there is no passage for water from the outer skin to the inner wallboard, making the caravan highly Resilient to moisture.

TESTED
Extensive safety and durability Testing at the Millbrook track, and cold chamber Testing down to minus 15°C and beyond puts prototypes through conditions most products will never have to experience in a lifetime; all part of the Swift Ethos to deliver the best products to you.

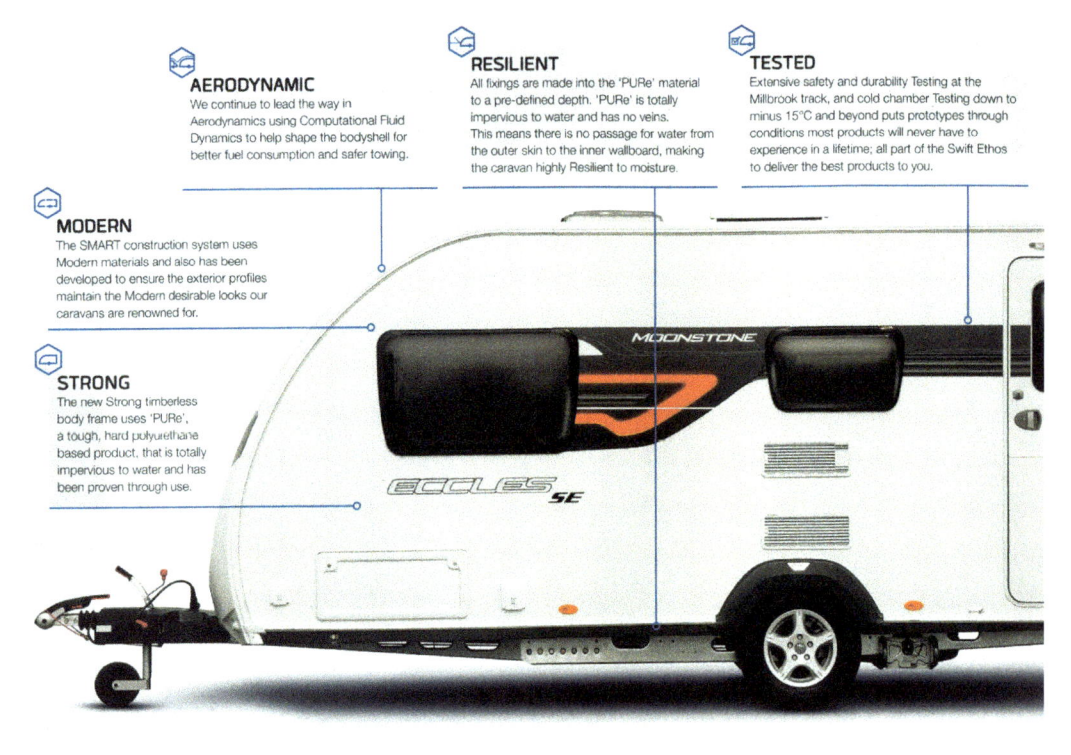

MODERN
The SMART construction system uses Modern materials and also has been developed to ensure the exterior profiles maintain the Modern desirable looks our caravans are renowned for.

STRONG
The new Strong timberless body frame uses 'PURe', a tough, hard polyurethane based product, that is totally impervious to water and has been proven through use.

The Eccles SE showing the benefits of SMART construction over timber.

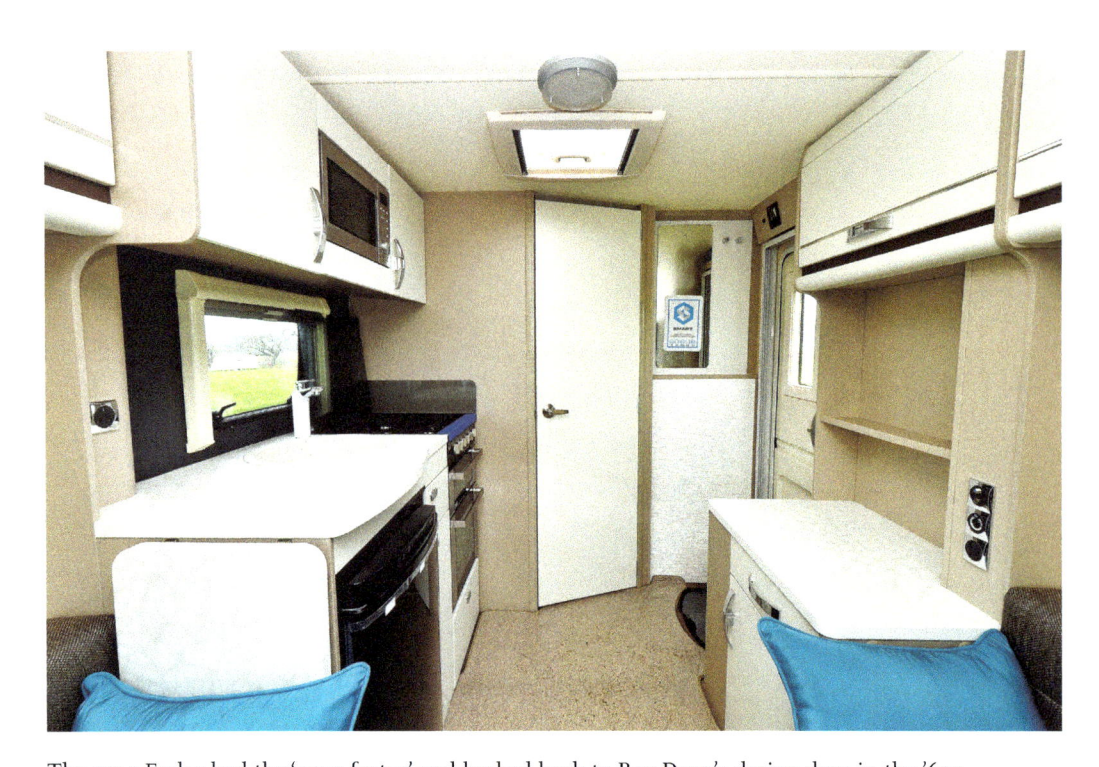

The 2014 Eccles had the 'wow factor' and harked back to Reg Dean's design days in the '60s.

The new construction was the biggest advance since Eccles' new sandwich-injected construction in 1976 in the old Ci days; Eccles again proved that the brand was always ahead of the game.

The 2014 line-up was carried through to 2015 but for 2016 the Eccles Sports were replaced by a standard yet restyled Eccles range; the SE line-up had gone and moved basically up to the Elite range, which didn't carry the Eccles badge, so again being a separate line-up. The new Eccles had eight layouts for 2016 but by 2017 the Eccles sported a new carbon-look front end panel plus Alde heating was offered as an option. The construction also included the Swift Group's honeycombed sandwich floor.

The Eccles SE interior from 2015 and twin single bed layout with rear-end washroom.

The 2016 Eccles were redesigned outside with a new, more curved front shell. Model names were dropped and replaced with numbers.

93

Contemporary interior has proved a top selling point for 2017 Eccles tourers, carrying on that innovative Eccles tradition.

The 2017 Eccles received carbon gloss-look front ends and Alde fitted as an order option.

What of the future?

On the 50th anniversary of Eccles in 1969, it was thought that this could be the possible Eccles in 2019! Sketched by Tom Karen of Ogle Design, he predicted it could be amphibious – now there's a thought!

Eccles ninety-eight years on is still innovative in many ways. It's hard to believe that the Rileys back then had the vision that would lead in many ways to Eccles being still a leading touring caravan brand in 2017. In 2019, the Eccles name will celebrate 100 years in production and the oldest name in the industry, and not just in the UK. On the 50th anniversary the then Ci group Eccles design, with the help of Tom Karen from Ogle Design, looked ahead to 2019; not quite as they predicted, but one thing for sure was that the Eccles name was still ahead in design and new construction. Eccles under the Swift Group's umbrella is an innovative brand and one that the Rileys and Sam Alper would be proud of.

Eccles, the oldest name in the business and known throughout Europe and beyond, is a testament to that original idea, that a car-pulled trailer caravan could become one of the most popular leisure lifestyles of the modern age.